BY VED MEHTA

Face to Face

Walking the Indian Streets

Fly and the Fly-Bottle

The New Theologian

Delinquent Chacha

Portrait of India

John Is Easy to Please

Daddyji

Mahatma Gandhi and His Apostles

The New India

Mamaji

The Photographs of Chachaji

A Family Affair

VEDI

Vedi, Murree Hills, 1943

VED MEHTA

VEDI

Oxford University Press

NEW YORK 1982 OXFORD

Copyright © 1981 by Ved Mehta

Library of Congress Cataloging in Publication Data

Mehta, Ved, 1934–
Vedi.

Text originated in The New Yorker.
Continues: Daddyji. 1972. and Mamaji. 1979.
1. Mehta, Ved, 1934–   2.   Blind—India—
Biography.   3.   Blind—Education—India.   I.   Title.
HV2093.M43A35   1982   362.4'1'0924 [B]   82-7902
ISBN 0-19-503005-2   AACR2

The contents of this book originated in The New Yorker

Printing (last digit) 9 8 7 6 5 4 3 2 1

Printed in the United States of America

To Pom, Nimi, and Umi

This is the story of my early education in an Indian orphanage for the blind, and, by extension, perhaps the story of the education of blind children elsewhere. But it is also a continuation of two earlier books— "Daddyji," a biographical portrait of my father, and "Mamaji," a biographical portrait of my mother—since the three volumes are all part of a series I am writing about my family and myself. As it happens, some of the experiences in "Vedi" I have touched upon in my first writings. That, however, was before I had quite found my voice as a writer and before I had acquired even the rougher implements of the craft. It was also before I had realized that memory expands by some kind of associative process, so that a remembered scene that at first seems hardly worth a line grows in the act of thinking and writing into a chapter, and this full-blown memory uncovers other memories, other scenes, which in their turn expand and multiply.

I wish to thank the Ford Foundation for a Public Policy Grant that allowed me to work on "Vedi." Also, in writing this book and preparing it for publication I was helped, in ways that only I can know and appreciate, by Judith Brudnick, Naomi Grob, and Lilla Pearce Weinberger. Here I can do no more than acknowledge their help and express my gratitude.

V. M.

New York
March 1982

P H O T O G R A P H S

Vedi, Murree Hills, 1943 / frontispiece

Family group, Simla, 1934 / 138

CONTENTS

I

ORPHANAGE

I REMEMBER THE TRAIN WHISTLE. IT BLEW WITH A rush of steam. Hurriedly, Daddyji drew my palms together within his own huge ones, said the Hindu farewell, *"Namaste,"* lifted me through the compartment window, and handed me to Cousin Prakash. "You are a man now," he said. This sentence of my father's was to become the beginning of my clear, conscious memory. In later years, I would recall it again and again, as if it were the injunction of my destiny. Cousin Prakash held me out just in time for Mamaji to kiss me before the train started moving.

What Daddyji would later remember about my going away in the train was the chill of the February day. Mamaji, however, would remember that she was oblivious of the cold as she held me tight against her chest at the station and felt my tears streaming down her neck; I seemed to sense that something awful was about to happen to me. "Vedi's not yet five," she said to Daddyji. "He's too young for a blind school."

"Do you want him always to be holding on to your sari?" he asked. "Or do you want him to make something of himself?"

She remembers that her impulse was to say, "I don't know if I want Vedi to make anything of himself," but she was a Hindu wife, and so she said nothing more. The train was hooting.

I remember that I didn't really understand until the train was moving forward—going ever faster, and getting more regular-sounding through the open windows—that I was going away. I called for Mamaji and Daddyji. I cried. I slept. I forgot. I remembered. I kicked against the leather berth. I banged my fists against the compartment wall. I cried. I slept. I woke to hear Cousin Prakash say, out of nowhere, "This is an express train, Vedi."

Cousin Prakash was a son of Daddyji's only sister. He was going to Bombay to try his hand at writing scripts for the cinema—he kept on calling me, affectionately, Actor. He loved Daddyji as he loved his own father, and my brother and sisters and I all thought of him as a brother. He was fond of me, but he didn't like looking after me; a bachelor, he didn't know what to do with a small child. I'd never been alone with him before, and I didn't like being with him on the train. He would say "Actor, why are you crying?" and "Actor, do you want to go to the bathroom?" and "Actor, would you like a glucose biscuit?" I couldn't say why I was crying, but I always wanted to go to the bathroom and I always wanted a glucose biscuit.

I remember that we were on the train for a day and a night and more. The air blew in through the open windows, covering my clothes, my hair, my berth with more and more grit and soot let fly by the engine. I remember that at one station Cousin Prakash bought me, through the open window, a packet of anise seeds coated with sugar. I remember thinking how much I liked him, and feeling happy in a surge.

At the Victoria Terminus in Bombay, we took a closed tonga, which Cousin Prakash called a victoria. I had never been in a closed tonga, and I asked him why the tonga and the station had the same name, but he was busy reading a newspaper and didn't answer.

I tried to pull the newspaper from his hand. "Daddyji explains everything!" I cried, and I begged him to take me home. But he ignored me.

Finally, he said, brushing the train soot off his clothes, "School, Actor—they'll teach you there how to read and write. You'll be very happy in the nice school."

As he spoke, the victoria slowed down. "This is the area, Sahib," the victoriawallah said.

Cousin Prakash, as he later told me, was mildly surprised to see that Dadar was a low-lying industrial area with open drains. It appeared to consist of dirty tenements, small, rickety wooden market stalls, and two gigantic textile mills. The mills were surrounded by seemingly impregnable stone walls—broken only by heavy iron gates and topped with barbed wire—and had tall chimneys billowing smoke. In fact, there was such a sooty smell in the air that Dadar could have been just another compartment in a train.

As Cousin Prakash later told it, the victoriawallah almost drove past the school, because he took it for a tenement. The school—a narrow, three-story structure of dark-gray stone with a small bird's nest of a tower— was wedged between the two mills and stood opposite some crumbling brick tenements, and laundry was hanging out of its windows. But the victoriawallah managed to bring the victoria to an abrupt stop just past the front of the school. We got down, and Cousin Prakash told the victoriawallah to wait. Even then,

Cousin Prakash says, he was not sure that we had been brought to the right place. But then, looking up, he saw a plaque next to a gate and read this:

To the Glory of God
Opened January 15, 1920
by
H. E. The Hon. Lady Lloyd
This Institution for the
Blind Standing on a Site
Provided by Government
Was Built from Funds Given
In Equal Proportions by
Many Interested Friends &
The Government of Bombay
Superintendent Miss A. L. Millard
Architectors Messrs Gregson
Batley and King
Clerk of the Works Mr. T. Gangaram

Inside the gate and just a few steps across a postage stamp of a courtyard was a veranda. On it I heard the clatter of brass utensils being pushed away against the bare floor and the rustle of people getting up. Several male voices said something to us in a language I didn't understand. (It was Marathi, the language of Bombay.) It sounded funny, like baby talk, and yet the voices were cracked and raspy, like those of some scary goblins I had once encountered at the Exhibition Ground in Lahore. ("You are a man now" was a gleaming memory, but there were other, wordless memories.)

"Why do they speak in that strange way?" I asked Cousin Prakash.

"He is bold," someone said, in broken Hindustani. I spoke Punjabi, but I could understand Hindustani, which I had heard at home from servants and venders.

"He's a new student," Cousin Prakash said, in Hindustani. Many hands reached out and touched me, almost tickling me in their welcome.

Cousin Prakash asked the boys on the veranda if this was their tiffin hour.

They answered in a jumble.

"It's Saturday."

"We have a long tiffin hour."

"It's tiffin hour."

"Where is your American-trained principal, Mr. Ras Mohun?" Cousin Prakash asked.

A boy took us up a flight of stairs, to a smaller veranda, and showed us into a room opening off it.

A man with a high-pitched voice, almost like Mamaji's, bent down and said something to me in another language I didn't understand. (The man was Mr. Ras Mohun, and he was speaking English.)

Mr. Ras Mohun, as he later recalled, hadn't thought that when it came down to it my parents would actually send me to his school. He could not quite believe that people of class and position, like my parents, would send a totally blind child of scarcely five to a school in a city thirteen hundred miles away—with a strange language, a strange climate, strange food—on the basis of a perfunctory correspondence, in which the question of how a well-to-do Punjabi child would survive in a Marathi-speaking orphanage (the school had about forty destitute boys and girls of all ages, most of them without known parents) was barely touched upon. Then he saw me walk into his sitting-and-dining room—the room off the upper veranda—with Cousin Prakash. Mr. Ras Mohun was struck by how much I looked like a normal, sighted boy, and for a moment he thought I must be not the boy intended for his school but a sighted son of Cousin Prakash. Even after I was introduced, he continued to believe that I had some sight, because, he says, he'd never before seen such normal-looking eyes and such an open, cheerful expression on the face of a blind child.

"The boy has a very winning smile," Mr. Ras Mohun said, in funny Hindustani.

I didn't know that he was talking about me till I felt a lady (Mrs. Ras Mohun) gather me up and heard her exclaim, "What a winning smile you have, Vedi!"

Cousin Prakash recalls that he looked at me but couldn't see what was special about my smile. All the same, he was satisfied that the Ras Mohuns were a good sort. He had had some reservations about them ever since Daddyji told him that they were Bengalis and Christians, because Cousin Prakash was a little wary of both.

Mr. Ras Mohun, taking no further notice of me, began to talk to Cousin Prakash in English.

Cousin Prakash said something quickly to the Ras Mohuns, and then, before I knew it, he was gone. He says that he was afraid I might cry and make a scene, which he thought would be awkward for everybody. He therefore slipped away without letting me know.

"Where is he?" I asked.

I had lost a front milk tooth in the train, and I couldn't talk properly. The words came out sounding thick, as if something were stuck to the roof of my mouth. I started crying.

"Mr. Anand is gone," Mr. Ras Mohun said, in faltering Hindustani. He used Cousin Prakash's surname, and for a moment I didn't know whom he meant. "I'm your uncle and this is your auntie," he continued.

"You're not," I said. "My uncles and aunties are in Lahore, at the train station."

"What a nice-looking boy you are!" Mrs. Ras Mohun said, kissing the top of my head. "You must come to your auntie just as you would go to your mummy."

"Yes," Mr. Ras Mohun said. "You will stay with us, and you will eat with us—we will take care of you."

Mrs. Ras Mohun set me down, and Mr. Ras Mohun took me by the hand and said, "Come along."

Mr. and Mrs. Ras Mohun led me out of the room, turned left, and walked a few steps. Mr. Ras Mohun unlocked a door and pushed it back. It sounded as if it were falling down. "It's falling," I said, through my tears.

They laughed.

"It's a metal accordion gate to the tower," Mr. Ras Mohun said. "Feel it."

I became very much interested. I had never before felt a gate that folded and unfolded like the bellows of a harmonium. For the time being, I forgot that Cousin Prakash had gone. I wanted to open and close the gate. But Mrs. Ras Mohun said, "Don't do that—you'll get your fingers caught."

We turned left again and walked through the gate. Mr. Ras Mohun closed it behind us. We climbed a flight of narrow stairs.

"Here is our daughter, Heea," Mrs. Ras Mohun said, taking me over to a crib. I put my hand into it and felt two kicking legs. They were Heea's. She was just a year old. She took hold of my finger and put it in her mouth. Again, I forgot for the time being that Cousin Prakash had gone.

❦

I SLEPT that night on a cot next to Heea's crib. In the morning, Heea's ayah told me that I couldn't use Mr. and Mrs. Ras Mohun's bathroom, and took me to the small children's bathroom; to get to it, we had to go downstairs and walk through the sitting-and-dining room to the other side of the building. The ayah had me sit under a tap. The water was cold and came out in a strong jet, making me shiver all over. I howled. I begged for a bucket of hot water and a dipper, as at home, so that I could wet myself slowly.

The ayah held me fast under the tap and said, "Come on now, Vedi, be a brave boy."

"No, I don't want to!" I cried.

"It's just like going out in the rain," she said.

I thought a moment, and then laughed.

The ayah let go of me.

"Rain, rain!" I yelled, and I turned on the tap full blast. The water poured out in a heavy stream and splashed all around me on the cement floor.

I ran to the ayah, who wrapped me in a little towel.

"Brave boy," she said, hugging me.

❦

AT BREAKFAST, in Mr. Ras Mohun's sitting-and-dining room, Mrs. Ras Mohun put my chair next to hers at a small, squarish table, tied a bib around my neck, and showed me how to eat a soft-boiled egg by myself with a spoon. I tried to get her to spread the egg on the toast, as Mamaji did at home.

"That's how jungly boys eat," Mrs. Ras Mohun said. "You must learn to eat your egg from its shell with a spoon."

"Vedi will be excused from the class of caning chairs," Mr. Ras Mohun said just as I started beating the shell with the spoon to make the opening bigger. "Caning chairs is for the poor boys, and he's a rich boy."

I didn't know what Mr. Ras Mohun was talking about, but as I beat the egg with the spoon I imagined that caning chairs was a game in which poor boys were given canes to beat a chair with. I was angry that Mr. Ras Mohun was not going to let me play the game, and wanted to run to Cousin Prakash and tell him.

"Cousin Prakash!" I cried. "I want to go to him!"

Mr. Ras Mohun tried to comfort me, but Mrs. Ras Mohun said, "Just ignore him."

I let go of the spoon and got soft-boiled egg on the tablecloth and on my bib.

"Only naughty boys throw their eggs around," Mrs. Ras Mohun said.

Mr. Ras Mohun tried to show me how to hold the spoon steady. Then he left, and Mrs. Ras Mohun washed my hands and face with water poured from a jug into a basin.

There was a thin, sharp, insistent sound from downstairs.

"What is that?" I asked, getting interested.

"What—that? That's Uncle's hand bell," Mrs. Ras Mohun said. "He is calling the boys and girls to the morning class."

"Where are the girls?"

"The girls live in the girls' dormitory, and the boys live in the boys' dormitory."

Mr. Ras Mohun returned and took me downstairs to the main classroom, where he left me with the school's Matron.

"Where do you live?" I asked her.

"In the girls' dormitory."

The Matron showed me a sort of wooden frame with a lot of beads on it. She counted the beads row by row, having me follow her fingers with my fingers and say the numbers after her. I got up to eighteen. I liked the way a mere touch could make the beads spin, and thought this was a nice game.

After a while, I knew that Mr. Ras Mohun was coming, because I recognized his walk—short, quick footsteps that click-clicked on the bare floor.

"It's lunchtime," he said, taking me by the hand. "Come along."

"I want to go there," I said, and I pulled him in the direction of the veranda, from which came the sounds of brass utensils on the bare floor and of boys laughing and talking.

He laughed. "They are poor orphans. Come. Auntie is waiting for us upstairs."

❦

ONE MORNING, a few days after my arrival, Mrs. Ras Mohun was sitting at her dressing table.

"What are you doing?" I asked.

"I am putting some cream and powder on my face."

"Can I have some?"

She bent down and put a big dab of cold cream on my face.

"More," I said.

She laughed. She covered my whole face with cream and rubbed it in.

"Some powder, too."

She laughed again. "Is that what your mummy did to you, Vedi?"

I had to stop and think, and then I remembered how I liked to climb into Mamaji's lap and feel her hands as she rubbed cream and powder into my face until I smelled like her.

I tried to climb into Mrs. Ras Mohun's lap, but she pushed me away. "Go wash your hands and face," she said.

"I want more, Auntie."

"Go away and wash," she said. "Powder and cream may not cost money in your rich home, but here they cost lots of money."

"How much?"

"Lots of money."

"Tell Ayah to give me my bath!" I yelled.

"The ayah is busy with Heea," Mrs. Ras Mohun said. "You're a big boy now. You have to learn to take your own bath."

"I want Ayah."

"You were spoiled at home," she said. "There is no

special ayah for you here. You have to learn to do
things by yourself."

Heea started crying. Mrs. Ras Mohun ran to her. I
followed, and tugged at Mrs. Ras Mohun, but she
would not stop tending to Heea.

MANY YEARS later, Daddyji told me how it happened that he sent me to Mr. Ras Mohun's school.
"When you lost your sight, I didn't know anything
about the blind," he said. I was hardly four when, in
the winter of 1938, I was left blind from meningitis.
"Like anyone else, I had, of course, often seen blind
people stumbling along, groping their way down a city
street. They usually carried a staff in one hand and a tin
cup in the other. Also, as a public-health officer, I had
visited many villages and seen blind villagers being
cared for by the joint-family system, which in those
days took in any and all relatives. But all those blind
people lived little better than wounded animals. I made
up my mind that my blind son would never have to de-
pend on the charity of relatives. I wanted you to be in-
dependent, like your sisters and brother. I wanted you
to be able to hold your head high in any company. I
started looking around for a school for you, and was
told that there were hardly a score of schools for the
blind in the whole country, and that the two or three
best ones were in Calcutta and Bombay. Calcutta was
out of the question. The Black Hole doesn't suit us
Punjabis. But I immediately placed advertisements in
the agony columns of newspapers in Bombay. That's

how I happened to hear from Mr. Ras Mohun, of Dadar School for the Blind.

"Mr. Ras Mohun wrote me that he was young, that he was married, and that he had a year-old daughter, and from this I surmised that he was a good family man. He said that he was a Christian and America-returned, and from this I concluded that he would not have the fatalistic attitude of our Hindu brethren, who regard blindness as a curse, and also that he would be conversant with progressive, Western methods of educating the blind. I wrote to Mr. Ras Mohun that I knew that the food and accommodations at his school would probably not be up to the standard of our home, and therefore I wondered if you could go to his school but live and board with him. I told him that, provided he could educate you, money would be no object. Mr. Ras Mohun wrote back to say that he would treat you like his own son, and that the expenses for room and board with him would come to forty rupees a month. As it happened, we were paying seventy-five rupees for your brother Om in Bishop Cotton School in Simla, and that was one of the top boarding schools. So I imagined that your room and board would be comparable, because Bombay was probably much cheaper than Simla.

"At first, your dear mother did not pay much attention to my efforts to find a school for you. She was trying all kinds of quack remedies—various eyedrops—that faith healers told her would make you see. Anyhow, she thought that, as always, I was writing letters, planning, and dreaming. When I told her about my determination to send you to Mr. Ras Mohun's school, she started crying that she could not let you go, and you started crying that you would not go. I remember that she asked me, 'What caste is Ras Mohun Sahib?' I laughed right out. 'You mean Mr. Ras Mohun? He's a Christian. He has no caste.' It was then that I learned from her that she put the blame for your blindness on the evil influence of the Christian wife whom Romesh" —Daddyji's younger brother—"had brought home around the time of your sickness. Many were shocked that Romesh had secretly married outside his caste and religion, and Bhabiji"—Daddyji's mother—"almost died from the shock, but I had no idea that your dear mother, in her superstitious way, had connected one event with the other. From the coincidence of time, she had somehow arrived at a relationship of cause and effect.

"Looking back, I blame myself for not having gone to the school and seen for myself the conditions there. But in those days Bombay seemed very far. Sometimes I wonder why Prakash didn't tell me, but, to be fair to him, he had no idea what schools for the blind were supposed to be like, and he formed a good impression of Mr. and Mrs. Ras Mohun. Anyway, I had made all the arrangements, and he felt that when he left you at the school he had done his duty."

DADAR SCHOOL, one of the first two or three schools for the blind in the country, got its start during the famine of 1900, when an American missionary, Miss Anna Millard, rounded up a few blind, hungry orphan boys and girls from the Bombay streets and took the responsibility of feeding them. She was a member of the American Marathi Mission, and she appealed to the sympathies of Bombay businessmen and the Bombay municipal authorities, who gave her some money. On a street called Love Lane, she established an orphanage—part home, part school—for the children and started teaching them English Braille; there was no accepted standard Braille for Indian languages. She also taught the older orphan boys to cane chairs, to weave wicker hampers for soiled clothes, and to hammer together simple objects, so that they could help defray some of the expenses of the place. But she paid the most attention to teaching the orphans hymns and the Bible, in the hope that they could go back to the streets one day as "blind Bible men" and "blind Bible women"—lay preachers. A pamphlet put out by the American Marathi Mission at that time notes:

> One of the most pathetic sights on the streets of many an Indian town is the blind beggar. He does not remain there except so long as he actually succeeds in securing alms. Cases have been reported in which ignorant, shiftless, cruel Indian parents have sometimes deliberately put the juice of a scalding herb into the eyes of an unpromising child so as permanently to blind the child, in the expectation that the blind child by begging alms would bring more of an income into the family than he would otherwise earn. . . .
>
> In marked contrast with such conditions is the life of the children who have been gathered into the school for the Blind [in Love Lane]. . . . The bright happy faces and the spontaneous testimony of the pupils in this school seemed to show that they have fulfilled to a higher degree than do

many seeing persons the prophecy (Revelation 22.4) which has been adopted as the motto of the school: "And they shall see His face."

This is an excellent instance of how the inspiration of Jesus of Nazareth, who healed and helped blind beggars in Palestine, has led to the transformation of some of the helpless blind children of India, who otherwise would be parasites on human society, so that they are happy persons, whose minds are filled with progressive knowledge, their mouths with gratitude for the love of God, and their hands with practical helpfulness.

Miss Millard sometimes took some of the objects made in the school's workshop to a charity bazaar and sold them, to good effect. An early American Marathi Mission report on the school notes, "One lady bought a footstool and took it home. She showed it to her son, who has charge of similar work in the Thana Jail. He said that the work compared favorably with that done by seeing men at the Jail."

Health conditions at the school, however, left something to be desired. Despite the care of a succession of Christian doctors, who provided their services free of charge, a number of Miss Millard's orphans seem to have died. (To quote the report, "Two of the girls have gone to 'look on His face,' in the words of the 'Glory Song' which the children love to sing.")

In 1920, the school was moved to a new building in Dadar. It occupied a little over half an acre. In due course, Miss Millard hired a couple of teachers. Then, in 1931, Mrs. Ross Thomas took charge of the school as superintendent. She and her husband had come to India as missionaries three years earlier, after joining the

American Marathi Mission in Boston, Massachusetts; she had worked with the blind at the Perkins Institution, in nearby Watertown, which was considered one of the most advanced centers for such work. She ran Dadar School mainly by visiting it now and then, until 1938, when she became the mother of a son. In that year, she appointed Mr. Ras Mohun the first resident principal.

Mr. Ras Mohun had been raised in the province of Bengal. At college, he had come under the influence of Christian missionaries, who used to take him along on field trips among the deaf and the blind. As a result, he had become interested in the work for the blind and had studied for a time at Perkins, like Mrs. Thomas. When he was thirty-one, he had married; his wife was a Bengali and was the same height he was. Two years later, their only child, Heea, was born.

Mr. Ras Mohun was overjoyed at his appointment. He received a good salary—two hundred and twenty-five rupees a month—along with a rent-free flat on the premises, consisting of the sitting-and-dining room and the sleeping quarters just above it, in the tower. Mrs. Ras Mohun, however, had no interest in the work for the blind and did not relish the thought of being cooped up in an orphan asylum situated between huge, smoky mills. "When we first came to the school, I saw this gloomy building of sooty stone and I wanted to bolt," she recalls. "There wasn't a single electric light in the building; apparently, the missionaries didn't see any need for lights in a school for the blind. The school had only one hurricane lamp, and that belonged to the Matron. When it got dark, she used to go around with her lamp and check that every bed had one person in it. Luckily, the school building had many facing windows. I opened them all up to help circulate the air. I also planted a few flowers in the back courtyard. We set to work to persuade the missionaries to give us lights. Eventually, we prevailed, but at first they installed only one light—in our sleeping quarters. At the time, there was hardly a month when someone didn't get sick and die. The place had no regular source of funds, no regular hours, no books, no syllabus of any kind. The small staff did little more than keep the animal urges of the boys and men in check."

Years later, Mr. Ras Mohun told me that he sometimes felt guilty at not having told Daddyji about Victoria Memorial School for the Blind, which was also in Bombay. Unlike Dadar School, which depended on fickle public charity (the cost of running it was about thirteen thousand rupees, or about forty-three hundred dollars, a year), Victoria School, founded in memory of Queen Victoria, was well endowed. It had a big three-story building, with open lawns, on a healthful site, and it accepted only children who were of the right age and were demonstrably educable. But then, Mr. Ras Mohun said, as an America-returned Indian Christian he took pride in the fact that Dadar School gave opportunity without discrimination to all of Christ's blind flock, and was in the best Christian tradition of education for the blind. He said he could never forget that the first school for the blind in the country had been established not by the government but by a Christian missionary, Miss Annie Sharp, as recently as 1887, and that the score or so of schools established since then were by and large

Christian in foundation. He felt that Dadar School could hold its head up among all of them, with the exception of Victoria School, and he told himself that I was one of the lucky few of the million or so blind people in the country who had a school to go to at all. (The Western practice of admitting blind students into sighted schools was almost unknown.) "I felt that under the circumstances you were better off at my school, under my guidance, than you would have been at Victoria School, which might have been more desirable from a worldly point of view but might not have provided the moral education that I knew you would get with us," he said.

II

BOYS'
DORMITORY

A FTER I HAD STAYED WITH MR. AND MRS. RAS MOHUN for a week, Mrs. Ras Mohun said to me at dinner, "Our sleeping quarters are too small. You'll be better off staying in the boys' dormitory with the other fellows."

"Shouldn't we really write to Dr. Mehta first?" Mr. Ras Mohun asked.

"Dr. Mehta is well-to-do," Mrs. Ras Mohun said. "If he knew the size of our sleeping quarters, he would understand."

"The beds in the boys' dormitory are not suitable for a well-to-do boy," Mr. Ras Mohun said. "But I suppose we can provide for a special bed for Vedi. Of course, he will continue to take his breakfast, lunch, tiffin, and dinner with us in our sitting-and-dining room. I suppose that if he is to amount to anything he must live with the other blind boys. The worst thing that can happen to blind children is to have overfond care."

"Where is it?" I said. "I don't want to go there."

"It's just through the door," Mr. Ras Mohun said. "The boys' dormitory is on this side of our sitting-and-dining room, beyond the boys' staircase, which you go up and down. The girls' dormitory is on the other side, beyond the girls' staircase."

"I'll stay upstairs with Heea," I said.

A day or two after this conversation, Mr. Ras Mohun took my hand and walked me a few steps from the sitting-and-dining room to the boys' dormitory, on the other side of the boys' staircase. Here he called over a boy who was twice my height, and said, "Vedi, this is your loving big brother Deoji. He will look after you."

I clung to Mr. Ras Mohun's leg. "He is not my brother!" I cried. "I want to stay with Heea."

Mr. Ras Mohun shook his leg free. I heard the click-click of his retreating footsteps. Before I could run after him, I heard the crashing sound of the metal accordion gate being closed, and he was gone.

Deoji bent down and pulled my cheeks—he had small, cold hands—and said, in faltering Hindustani, "What nice fat cheeks you have. You must come from the house of very well-to-do people."

"I want to go to Heea! I want to go to Uncle and Auntie!" I cried.

"Are you totally blind?" Deoji asked.

"I can't see," I said, and I pulled him toward the accordion gate. "Take me to Uncle and Auntie."

"I am partially sighted," he said, taking my face between his hands.

"I want to go to Heea."

"Heea can't talk. You'll have a good time here in the boys' dormitory."

He sat me down on a sort of platform a little way inside the room.

"What is this?" I asked, running my hands all around the platform. It consisted of a few bare boards laid side by side on top of a heavy iron frame.

"This is my bed. You can play on it. You don't have a bed yet, but they are going to bring one. It's going to be a special spring bed with a mosquito net."

Deoji showed me around the boys' dormitory. It

was a long room lined with two rows of beds like his, with a narrow passageway between.

Suddenly, there were the shouts and rough laughter of boys running into the room.

Deoji said something to them in Marathi.

"Hold him up!" a few boys shouted, in broken Hindustani. "Let the partially sighted see!"

Deoji lifted me up and then put me down.

Many boys scrambled forward and touched me all over. They kept touching my cheeks.

"What fat cheeks he has!" one exclaimed.

"How round his cheeks are!" someone else said.

A boy started tugging at my clothes. "His clothes are soft and pressed."

Deoji tried to push the boys along, but they wouldn't move.

Several of the boys clasped my hands in their rough ones.

"What soft hands he has!" one boy said.

"He has soft hands like a girl's," another said.

One boy caught hold of both my hands and exclaimed, "So smooth! Never had to work!" His rasping fingers went over my hands again and again, in disbelief. "What is your name?"

"Vedi."

"Vedi! A nickname for Ved?"

"Yes," I said.

"He's called that because he's small," someone else said.

I tried to pull away. The boy holding both my hands laughed and tightened his grip. "Why don't you laugh?" he suddenly asked me.

Everyone laughed.

"Leave him alone," Deoji said. "He's Mr. Ras Mohun's personal guest. Didn't you all hear how gently Mr. Ras Mohun spoke to him in the classroom yesterday?"

I heard again the clicking sound of Mr. Ras Mohun's shoes. "Mr. Shoes," someone said.

The boy let my hands drop. Everyone stepped back. There was an uneasy silence as the shoes clicked louder and louder. At that moment, I realized that since I entered the boys' dormitory I had heard the sound of no other shoes—only the sound of bare feet shuffling.

THAT EVENING, a special bed was wheeled in for me, and it was very different not only from the other boys' platformlike beds but also from the cots I had slept on at home and upstairs, in Mr. and Mrs. Ras Mohun's sleeping quarters. It had a smooth metal frame with railings at the head and the foot, metal poles from which a mosquito net was strung, a heavy mattress, and springs. It was placed between Deoji's bed and the corner bed, which was just inside the door and belonged to the Sighted Master. The Sighted Master was the head of the boys' dormitory and the only completely sighted person there.

The boys immediately dubbed my bed "the hospital bed." I didn't like the bed, and didn't want to get into it, even though it was bedtime. But Deoji lifted me in and tucked the mosquito net under the edges of the mattress.

"I want to go upstairs to Auntie!" I cried.

"You can be with me," Deoji said.

"I want to go to the bathroom," I said.

Deoji took me across the upper veranda, past the door of the sitting-and-dining room, and past the metal accordion gate, to a small room. "This is the boys' common bathroom," he said, showing me a hole in the floor and a tap. "You sit on this hole and go to the bathroom," he said.

"I'll fall in," I said, and I begged him to take me upstairs to Mr. and Mrs. Ras Mohun, who had a commode.

"I will hold you. It's all right."

I protested. "No! Upstairs with Auntie!"

I fought and cried, and then sat down as Deoji showed me.

Deoji again put me to bed. "You are our special boy," he said. "You have shoes and a mosquito net and a mattress. No one else in the boys' or girls' dormitory has such things. By the bye, what kind of beds do Mr. and Mrs. Ras Mohun have?"

I couldn't say, because I didn't know or I didn't remember. I always used to climb into Daddyji's bed or Mamaji's bed, but I never climbed into Mr. Ras Mohun's bed or Mrs. Ras Mohun's bed. "I think Heea sleeps in their cot," I said.

Deoji laughed. "Go to sleep," he said, and he went back to his bed.

I couldn't go to sleep. My bed was a little longer than the other beds and stuck out into the passageway, so the boys kept bumping into it as they went to the bathroom and came back.

I heard the sound of the metal accordion gate opening and the click-click of Mr. Ras Mohun's shoes. He walked energetically, as if he were saying to himself, "Left, right, left," and yet his step was so light that he might have been Mamaji in high heels. I heard the boys falling on top of their wooden beds, and in a moment the whole boys' dormitory was quiet.

"No one should make any noise," Mr. Ras Mohun said, in his shrill voice, coming in and flicking off the light switch, just like Mamaji at home. "I don't want to have to punish anyone with my ruler. I see the Sighted Master is already asleep." He left.

The bed was so big; the room was so large and so crowded. I cried. I slept. I woke up. All around, people were snoring and grinding their teeth. I pressed my face against the pillow to stop my howls.

I felt someone cautiously untucking the mosquito net.

I held my breath and lay very still. I thought that it was the Sighted Master, and that he was going to punish me. But he was snoring on the other side of my bed.

Someone put his head inside the mosquito net, and I heard Deoji's voice. "Vedi," he murmured.

I cried into the pillow and clung to it.

"The other boys will hear you," he said. "What will they think?"

He gathered me up with the pillow and carried me out of the boys' dormitory. He sat down on the top step of the boys' staircase, clumsily put me down next to him, and said, in a whisper, "You're only homesick. You miss your mummy. I cried, too, when they first brought me here. I missed my Foundling Home. But I soon forgot about it. In a few days, you'll forget about your mummy, and you'll like it here. We have a swing and a seesaw and climbing bars here. Are you good at climbing?"

"Where are they? I want to see."

"They're outside, in the back courtyard. It's night, and snakes will be out there now. I'll show you those things tomorrow." He pulled my cheeks.

I touched his face. It felt thin and taut and rough. I shrank back.

He laughed and pulled my cheeks again and asked me, "What do you call them in Punjabi?"

"*Galls,*" I said, laughing. The Punjabi word sounded very funny in front of Deoji.

"Say in Punjabi, 'I have a new loving big brother named Deoji.'"

"I don't want to."

"Please do."

I said it, and he repeated it after me.

"You sound like a duck," I said, and we both laughed.

"No, it is Mr. Ras Mohun who sounds like a duck," he said, in a barely audible whisper. We laughed even more.

"Why do you call Uncle Mr. Ras Mohun?" I asked.

"I'm too poor to call him Uncle. Besides, I don't have any uncles. I have no family, no relations. I am solitary."

"Who was it you stayed with when you were small?"

"I stayed with my missionary mummy and daddy."

"What are missionaries?"

"Missionaries? Missionaries? Well, you can say they are like Mr. and Mrs. Ras Mohun. Mr. and Mrs. Ras Mohun are your missionary uncle and auntie."

"How did you find your missionary mummy and daddy?"

"They told me that I had come to them as a little baby and that they had named me Deoji. Now I'm fifteen. I've been here for seven years. My missionary mummy and daddy sent me to this school when I was already eight."

"Where are your missionary mummy and daddy?"

"In their mission orphanage."

"Can I—"

"Sh-h-h. We've broken a strict rule by leaving the boys' dormitory. If the Sighted Master finds out and reports us, Mr. Ras Mohun will beat us with his ruler."

He took my hand, and we tiptoed back.

IN THE MORNING, Deoji helped me to make my bed. He showed me how to pull the mosquito net out from under the mattress on all sides and then straighten the sheets and tuck them and the mosquito net in tight. I was too small to lift the ends of the mattress by myself, and, in any case, my arms got tired. Also, try as I might, bunches of mosquito net hung down like shirt-tails. So Deoji did most of the work.

He then took me to the boys' common bathroom and said, "Now you have your wash under the tap."

"In the children's bathroom with Ayah!" I cried.

"That's for the little children who live on the girls' side," he said. "You are now with the big boys, in the boys' dormitory."

He handed me a chunk of soap. It was so big that my hand wouldn't go around it, and one end of it was ragged, as if it had been broken off from a bar of soap.

"I want my Pears' soap!" I yelled, remembering how Pears' soap smelled like Mamaji's hands, how it was oval, like the mirror of Daddyji's car, and how it fitted my small hand like a mango stone.

"I don't know what Pears' soap is, but this Lifebuoy is a very good soap," he said. "All the boys use it, and it keeps us free of boils."

The soap slipped out of my hand, but I rubbed what little soap had got on my hands onto my legs, and washed them with the cold water from the tap.

"Here is some hair oil," Deoji said, handing me a bottle. It was big and round and difficult to hold.

"It's the wrong bottle," I said, remembering a small, flat bottle of Vaseline Hair Tonic that I used at home.

He took the bottle from me and asked me to hold out my hand. He put some oil in my palm. The oil was thick and smelled bad.

"I don't like the smell! I want my Vaseline Hair Tonic!" I cried.

"This is a very good oil," he said. "It's the best. It's Tata Coconut Oil. All the boys use it, and it keeps lice away."

I put the oil on my head, and then sat down under the tap and washed myself all over.

Deoji showed me how to dry my back by myself—

by holding the towel behind me with both hands and running it back and forth. Then I wrapped the towel around me, and he took me back to the boys' dormitory and showed me some shelves against a wall. On the shelves were some boxes and my leather suitcase, which I had brought from home. He got down my suitcase and fetched from it a silk shirt, a pair of cotton knickers, a pair of socks. He showed me how to get into my clothes by myself—by holding on to the wall and balancing myself.

In subsequent days, Deoji introduced me to more and more of the boys: to Abdul, to Bhaskar, to Reuben, to Dham. They were continually coming up to me and pulling my cheeks and calling me "the little fellow with big cheeks." They said that Mr. and Mrs. Ras Mohun had shoes, as I did, and that they wore soft clothes, as I did, but that only I had fat Punjabi cheeks.

At five, I was the youngest boy in the boys' dormitory, and the other boys could not understand why I seemed so healthy: why they never heard me scratch my head, why I never coughed at night, why I never complained of a stomach ache in the morning—above all, why I never had a fever. The boys kept coming up and touching my forehead and exclaiming, "He still doesn't have a fever!"

I learned Marathi very quickly, and although the boys continued to pull my cheeks and feel my forehead, they forgot that I was a Punjabi.

One day when a button had come off my shirt, Deoji taught me how to thread a needle with a "threader"—a little coinlike thing with a wiry hook—

and how to knot the thread, then pluck out with my teeth the threads where the old button had been, and sew on a new button. He showed me how to scrape some polish from a tin onto a brush and then buff my shoes, feeling them all around to make sure that they felt clean. I was better at sewing than I was at polishing. No matter how careful I was, I always got polish on my clothes and in my hair; it seemed to fly through the air, like the soot from the mills next door.

Whatever progress I made, I never got used to going to the boys' common bathroom. It smelled so bad that I had to hold my nose when I was there. The floor was wet, and sometimes, if I wasn't careful, I would slip and fall. Wasps seemed to be always buzzing around the walls; I remember once I got too close to a corner, and a wasp stung me.

Deoji had told me about a bathroom ghost who lived inside the wall. "If anyone stays there too long, the bathroom ghost will pounce on him and bite off his nose," he had said. "If he ever attacks you, just pray to Jesus, Mary, and Joseph."

"Who are they? What will they do to the ghost?"

"Jesus, Mary, and Joseph live up in Heaven. They are very nice to the blind sort. Ghosts slide away just at the mention of their names."

Whenever I went to the bathroom, I could hear the ghost shift his weight from foot to foot; he made the whole bathroom wall shake. I always prayed to Jesus, Mary, and Joseph, and he didn't bother me.

I remember that many times I asked Mrs. Ras Mohun to let me use the bathroom upstairs in her sleeping quarters, but she always said, "How can you come upstairs? The gate to our sleeping quarters is closed at night. It's best that you go to the bathroom with the other big boys."

I didn't like my clothes any more than I liked going to the boys' common bathroom, but for a very different reason. I had many shirts and many pairs of knickers and many changes of socks. I could wear a different shirt, different knickers, different socks every day for two weeks. Heea's ayah, who did my laundry, once said to me, "I've never seen so many nice clothes." The boys were constantly coming up to feel my clothes and would coo over how soft and superior they were. But my clothes seemed to me like party clothes, because all the other boys wore rough-feeling short-sleeved shirts and rough-feeling knee-length pajamas. Also, the boys had just two changes of clothes each. They wore the same shirt and the same pajamas to school and to bed, and they wore them for a week, until the day of the washerman. On that day, the washerman waited while the boys got out of their soiled clothes and into the clean ones he had brought. If the washerman lost Deoji's shirt, Deoji had to wear his soiled shirt until the Sighted Master reported the loss to Mr. Ras Mohun and Mr. Ras Mohun got him a new shirt.

I remember that in the beginning I asked Deoji, "Why do you wear short-sleeved shirts and funny, short pajamas? Why is your cloth so rough—why does it feel like your rough cheek?"

"We are lucky, because the school is next to the Tata Mill, which gives Mr. Ras Mohun this cloth free of charge," he said. "It may be only Tata's waste cloth, but there are many orphanages and foundling homes begging for it. We are lucky to be here in the school and to have good Tata cloth for clothing."

After that, I wanted to wear a short-sleeved shirt and short pajamas, too, and go barefoot, like all the other boys. I remember once, when Deoji was helping me into my shoes, I cried, "I want to go barefoot, like you!"

"You are lucky to be well-to-do and have shoes," he said, buckling them up tight. "And soft clothes to wear, too."

"I won't wear them," I said.

"Mr. Ras Mohun says you must, and he has a ruler."

"What color shirt do I have on?" I asked.

"I don't know. I'm going blind."

"If my loving big brother Om were here, he could tell. You are not my loving big brother."

That day, I met Paran in the classroom.

"You have a nice blue shirt on," she said.

"How do you know?"

"I am half sighted. I can see your shirt four or five yards away."

"How old are you?" I asked.

"I am ten."

"Come up and eat toast with Uncle and Auntie and me," I said.

"I can't eat toast," she said. "I am only a poor orphan. I eat maize bread."

That night, I couldn't go to sleep. I kept thinking about Paran. I wondered why she couldn't eat toast and what kind of teeth she had. Deoji had once brought me a piece of the maize bread that the boys and girls ate, and I preferred it to toast; it was tastier, and it made me feel close to them. But it was so hard that I feared that eating it would break my teeth. Now a mosquito was buzzing around my head. I slapped my pillow, bounced on the bed, shook out the mosquito net, but the mosquito wouldn't go away. I began to wonder why I had to eat toast, like Mr. and Mrs. Ras Mohun, why I had to sleep in a hospital bed, why I had to wear soft clothes and go around in shoes. I thought that Daddyji would have let me eat what I liked, sleep where I liked, wear what clothes I liked, and go barefoot if I liked. I wished he were there, so I could ask him to arrange things. I started crying.

"What's the matter?" Deoji asked, opening the mosquito net and poking his head in.

"I want Daddyji and Mamaji," I said.

"But I am here."

"But you can't tell Uncle to excuse me from eating toast."

"But toast is nice sahib food."

I cried louder. "I don't want sahib food. I think Daddyji and Mamaji have forgotten me."

"Of course they haven't forgotten you. They are your mummy and—"

I had a fit of sneezing. In the next bed, the Sighted Master cleared his throat and muttered something. I was afraid that my sneezing would wake him up, but the sneezes kept coming, like the click-click of Mr. Ras Mohun's shoes.

The Sighted Master turned over, thrashing around

under his bed covers. But soon his breathing became regular.

Deoji whispered, "It's lucky for us that the Sighted Master sleeps like a deaf man. It's fine to sneeze. You know what it means when you sneeze?"

"What?"

"It means that someone in your family is thinking about you. I can't tell you who, but someone is surely remembering you."

"Does that mean that when I think about Daddyji and Mamaji, they sneeze, too?" I asked, between sneezes into my pillow.

"To be sure," he said.

I was excited by the thought and wanted to go on sneezing, even as I feared waking up the Sighted Master.

"Your mummy and daddy love you very much, or they wouldn't have spent so much money to send you here," Deoji was saying. "Do you know how much money they are spending per month?"

"How much?" I asked.

"You could buy all the caned chairs in the school and still have money left over."

The workshop downstairs was full of chairs with sagging and half-broken cane seats and backs, and some boys spent days cutting the caning out and weaving new, taut seats and backs, the pattern of holes so even that I couldn't work out how they did it. But I imagined that it cost the chairs' owners plenty of money.

Deoji went back to his bed. I heard a continuous muffled scratching near the shelves. "Deoji!" I whispered across to him. "What is that?"

"It's just a rat," he whispered back. "Go to sleep."

I tucked the mosquito net in tight around me and tried to sleep.

I dreamed that a big kitty had come into my mosquito net and was biting me. "New clothes, new clothes," she meowed, pretending that it was my birthday and that her bites were only birthday pinches. But whichever way I turned, there were her teeth. I woke up with a start.

I got down and shook Deoji and told him about the nasty kitty.

"Don't worry," he said. "That's just your soul having an adventure with the kitty. When you go to sleep, your soul leaves your body and goes on adventures of its own. It does the things it likes—the things you can't do. That's why I tell the boys always to wake up slowly —so that their souls have time to get back."

From downstairs came sounds—the clink of bangles in the kitchen, the echoes of little children reciting something in the classroom, the hubbub of girls eating their meal on the veranda.

"Deoji, Deoji, listen!" I whispered. "The bangles!"

"Oh, that," he said. "Those are ghosts. They go to school at night. They take over the downstairs of the building.

"Do they bite? Are they as big as the bathroom ghost?"

"They'll only hurt you if you disturb them. They are as light as an eyelash, and as slippery as the mercury of the broken thermometer that the Sighted Master used to have. They can float in and out of the school any time they like, but they prefer the dark. In the day, they generally live in the ghost castle. It's a big building just on the other side of the Tata Mill—without windows or doors, chimneys or drains."

I crept back to my bed and tucked the mosquito net in tight. I lay very still and prayed to Jesus, Mary, and Joseph to make the ghosts eat their meal quickly and finish their lessons and hurry away. I pressed my ear against my pillow and heard the ghost-cook in the kitchen below kneading and slapping dough and turning chapattis on the griddle.

She was sitting cross-legged on the kitchen floor. I went to her and sat down in her lap. She had fire tongs in her hand, and she was busy stoking the coals in the brick oven, but she patted my head with her free hand.

"Open your mouth," she said. "Let me see your teeth. Tch, tch, tch, they're all yellow. Here, hold out your hand." She put something in my hand with the fire tongs. It was hot and cold at the same time. "That's ash. Just put it in your mouth, and rub it around your teeth with your forefinger, and you'll have teeth as white as mine."

The ash tasted warm and crunchy and stuck to my teeth like toffee.

"I've got you! I've got you!" she cackled. "I'm taking you to the ghost castle!"

"No! No!" I cried, trying to fight her off.

I woke up. I ran my tongue around my teeth. I could feel no sticky ash. But in the middle of my bed there was a scary spreading patch of wetness.

III

UNCLE AND AUNTIE

O NE DAY AT THE TABLE, I TRIED TO GET THE ATTENtion of Mrs. Ras Mohun. "I want more potatoes, Auntie!" I shouted, as I would have shouted at home.

"You see I'm talking to Uncle, and you're interrupting," she said.

"But I want more potatoes now!" I shouted.

"You will get no potatoes until you learn manners," Mrs. Ras Mohun said.

I beat the table with my spoon. I pummelled Mrs. Ras Mohun's back. I pulled her hair, which was long and thick, like Mamaji's. I tried to climb onto the table to find the dish of potatoes.

But Mrs. Ras Mohun firmly pushed me back into my chair and said, "Don't be a jungly boy."

"I'll tell my sister Umi about you. She'll come and beat you up."

Mrs. Ras Mohun laughed, and then said sternly, "You are never to bang the table, never to pull anyone's hair, never to climb on the table. If you need more food, you are to raise your hand and hold up your fourth and little fingers and wait until I notice you. If I am talking to Uncle or looking after Heea, you are to keep your hand up and wait."

"I don't want potatoes anymore," I said. "I want water."

"When you want water, you should raise your hand and hold up just your little finger. Now let me see you do it."

I beat the table and shouted, but I did not get a glass of water until I sat quietly in my chair and raised my hand and held up my little finger.

Thereafter, whenever I remembered, I raised my hand, but sometimes I would get tired or angry holding up my hand while Mrs. Ras Mohun went on eating or talking. Then I would find myself beating the table with my spoon, or sulking and refusing to eat or drink.

"You think you can be a good child with manners one minute and become a jungly boy the next minute," Mrs. Ras Mohun would say. "That's just not possible. You have to discipline the jungly boy in you."

I remember that she also tried to break me of the habit of eating with my fingers, and tried to teach me to eat with a spoon. But I had trouble eating with the spoon. The food would scoot around the plate and slide onto the tablecloth. It wouldn't balance on the spoon, or it would fall off just as I got it up to my mouth, spraying me, the tablecloth, and sometimes Mrs. Ras Mohun with gravy.

One evening when I went in to dinner, Mrs. Ras Mohun had a separate small table set up for me, a little distance from the table at which she and Mr. Ras Mohun and Heea sat. After that, I always ate at the separate table, and whenever I remembered I used my fingers to signal for more food or water and ate with a spoon.

AT MEALS, Mr. and Mrs. Ras Mohun generally spoke Marathi to me, mixed in with a few Hindustani words whenever I couldn't understand, but spoke to each other in English. The only time I had heard English at home was when Daddyji was listening to the news on the radio, so I could understand little of what Mr. and Mrs. Ras Mohun said. One day, Mrs. Ras Mohun started teaching me English conversation. I remember that the first words were "chicken," "kitchen," and "thank you," and I had difficulty with all of them. I called chicken "kitchen" and kitchen "chicken" and said "tank you."

Whenever I asked for something in Marathi, Mrs. Ras Mohun would say, "You'll get it only if you ask for it in English."

"Why must I ask for things in English?" I once asked her.

"So that both Heea and you can grow up knowing English," Mrs. Ras Mohun said. "Uncle has great plans for her and you."

"Your father would like you to go to England and America, as he did, and study there," Mr. Ras Mohun said.

"Where are England and America?" I asked.

"They are far, far away," Mr. Ras Mohun said, "across the oceans and deserts."

After that, whenever I found Heea in the Ras Mohuns' sitting-and-dining room I would speak English to her. In fact, I decided I would take her along with me to England and America.

I REMEMBER I once asked Mrs. Ras Mohun for "starbries."

"What's that?"

"You know, starbries."

"That may be something in Punjabi, but what do you call them in Hindustani?"

"Starbries!"

"Is it a fruit or a vegetable?"

"Starbries!"

"Is it something you peel?"

"No."

"What does it taste like?"

"Like starbries!" I shouted.

"If you won't tell me what it is, how can you expect me to get it for you? Maybe it's something you have in the Punjab that we don't have in Bombay."

Not long after that, Mrs. Ras Mohun said to me, "I'm writing a letter to your daddy. Do you want anything from home?"

"Starbries," I said.

"Never you mind about that. Do you want anything else?"

"Yes. Tantra."

"Oh, not tantra again. I don't think there has been a single day when you haven't asked for it, even though you know perfectly well that we don't know what you're talking about. Tantra, starbries, starbries, tantra. I don't think I'll ever hear the end of them. But do you want to send love to anybody?"

"I don't love Sister Umi."

"But the only sister you ever talk about is Umi. Why is that?"

"She says she's Daddyji's favorite. But I'm Daddyji's favorite."

❦

As Daddyji and Mamaji remember it, the Ras Mohuns at first wrote to them quite regularly about my progress. Daddyji formed a good opinion of them from their letters. Mamaji, however, had her reservations—especially after Mrs. Ras Mohun's "tantra" letter.

"Mrs. Ras Mohun writes that every day the child asks for 'tantra,' and she doesn't know what it is," Daddyji said to Mamaji at the breakfast table, reading a letter that had just arrived in the post. "Mrs. Ras Mohun thinks Vedi must be asking for a Punjabi sweetmeat. He also seems to want what looks like 'strawberries.' "

"Every mother knows that children say 'tantra' for 'santra,' " she said. ("Santra" means "orange.")

He wasn't sure whether strawberries were available in Bombay, but he promised to write to Mrs. Ras Mohun and tell her about the santra.

That evening, before going to the club, he wrote:

My Dear Mrs. Ras Mohun,

Young Punjabi children often call "santra" "tantra." As you may know, the Punjab is called "the bread basket of India," because we send food to other parts of the country. We have many kinds of fruit here. Vedi loves—in addition to oranges and strawberries—mangoes, litchis, loquats, pomegranates, guavas, bananas. I appreciate that some of these fruits may not be easily obtained in Bombay, but I'm sure oranges are, and his dear mother and I will be indebted to you and Mr. Ras Mohun if Vedi could be given an orange after a meal now and again, and perhaps a glass of fresh orange juice in the morning.

He looked up from his writing paper. "Any message for Vedi?" he asked her.

"Tell him that I press him against my neck," she said.

He laughed. "Such things are hard to write in English," he said, and he wrote, "Tell Vedi that his dear mother sends her fondest love."

❦

"HERE'S A SANTRA for you," Mrs. Ras Mohun said at the table.

I was very excited, and reached out and grabbed it from her hand.

Santras as I remembered them were light and soft and had crinkly skins. They had an indentation at the top for my thumb. I could peel them without any difficulty. But the thing she handed me was heavy and hard. It had a smooth skin, almost like an egg. Instead of the indentation for my thumb, it had a little pimple. I was so disappointed that I almost threw it on the floor.

"It's not a tantra," I said. "It's something horrible."

"Of course it's a santra!" Mrs. Ras Mohun said, and she reached over and sliced it with a knife on my plate.

Under protest, I took a bite of a slice. It tasted like an orange, all right, but the skin wouldn't come off the juicy part.

"Give some of it to Heea," Mr. Ras Mohun said.

"She can have all of it," I said. "I don't want it."

"You have to eat it," Mrs. Ras Mohun said. "I went to a lot of trouble to get it for you."

I ate more of the orange. I began enjoying it, and I felt very happy.

Heea reached over and tried to take the slice of orange I was eating. I tried to hold on to it. She bit my hand with her few teeth. I scratched her face.

Mrs. Ras Mohun lifted me roughly off my chair and pushed me ahead of her up to her sleeping quarters. There she cut my nails with a big nail cutter. I tried to fight her off, but she held me fast between her knees.

"WE HAVE ONLY bitter gourd and bread tonight," Mrs. Ras Mohun said one evening when I went in for my dinner. "The bazaars are closed. There is a war on, and now there is a general strike on top of it." She put some bitter gourd on my plate.

I took a little spoonful of it. It had a pimply, slippery texture and a bitter, sharp taste. I left it on my plate.

"Eat it up," she said. "It's all there is, and it's good for you."

"I won't," I said, pushing the plate away.

"Here. Take this spoonful."

I sensed her hand with the spoon in it coming toward me. I closed my mouth tight.

"You will eat it."

"I won't. Never," I said through clenched teeth.

"Look how stubborn he is," she said to Mr. Ras Mohun.

He did not reply. He sat talking quietly to Heea.

Mrs. Ras Mohun marched me up to her sleeping quarters. She took gauze and wound it around each of my hands.

"I won't unwrap your hands until you agree to eat bitter gourd."

"I will get Deoji to feed me," I said angrily.

"Don't be impudent," she said. "Go to bed."

Hurriedly, I ran out of her sleeping quarters and down the narrow stairs and threw myself on my bed, repeating in my head, "I will not eat bitter gourd. I will not cry. I don't like her." I hooked my feet on the edge of the mattress and shook my bed, pretending that it was a train and was taking me away—far, far away from the school. I fell asleep.

When I woke up in the morning, I was surprised to feel that there were bandages on my hands. Mr. Ras Mohun had told some of the boys about my misbehavior, and word of it had spread through the boys' dormitory. Everyone got up and, without speaking to me, went to breakfast.

I did not cry. I stayed in bed, listening to Jaisingh, the deaf, dumb, and blind boy, moan and howl, until Mrs. Ras Mohun came and got me for my breakfast.

I didn't want to go, but I was hungry.

Mrs. Ras Mohun removed the gauze from my hands. Her fingers were soft and tender and smelled of nice soap. I could have eaten them.

ONE AFTERNOON, Mr. Ras Mohun took me to do some shopping. On the road, he suddenly stopped and said, "Let me see how you walk."

I didn't know why he was asking me that. I took a few steps.

"Just as I thought—you're not walking right," he said. "Touch my shoes and see how I walk."

Click-click, I thought, and I wondered if his shoes had high heels, like Mamaji's. I bent down and felt them all around; they were ordinary flat shoes, with laces, like Daddyji's.

"No, no, just feel the toes!" he called down to me. He started walking, and I hopped along at his side. "See how straight I walk—see how my toes point in. Now you try to walk like that."

I stood up and clung to his hand and walked every which way.

"No, no—not that way," he said, and he bent down, caught hold of my toes, and pushed them inward. "Keep your toes turned in, like this. Then lift your foot straight up, like this; then put your heel down, like this; then bring down your toe, like this."

I clutched at his short hair and tried to walk as he pointed and moved my feet, his voice rising from my shoes. "Left toe in. . . . Left foot up. . . . Left heel down. . . . Left foot forward. . . . Right toe in. . . . Right foot up. . . . Right heel down. . . . Right foot forward."

I felt as if I were going to fall, and cried out, "I can't!" But Mr. Ras Mohun paid me no attention. He held my shoes and hopped along at my side. I thought what a nice head of hair he had. It was soft, curly, and oily and smelled of coconut. I thought I might never learn to walk correctly but I would be sure to remember to massage my head the next day with Tata Coconut Oil.

"That's the way—left, right, left, right."

I suddenly remembered that that was the way Mr. Ras Mohun himself walked—my toes went out again.

"Try one foot at a time, and say to yourself, 'Left, right, left, right,' " Mr. Ras Mohun said.

I did, and that was much better, as long as I kept on repeating to myself, "Left, right, left, right."

Ahead, I heard a thundering clatter that I didn't recognize. I jumped, almost kicking his hands.

"It's the tram," Mr. Ras Mohun said. We ran and climbed on it.

I liked the tram's wobbling and roaring, the irregular rumbling of its wheels, and the constant ringing of a bell, which gave our ride a sense of speed and excitement.

"What's the bell? Why does it ring so much? Who rings it? I want to feel it!"

"The bell is to warn people in the street to get out of the way," Mr. Ras Mohun said. "But you can't touch it."

I remembered Daddyji and how he had once shown me a tonga. He had put my hands on the yoke, to show me how it rested on the horse; then in the horse's mouth, to show me how the bit was fitted between the teeth; then on the reins, to show me how the horse was controlled. He had let me feel the horse's tail to see how it was tucked in between the carriage and the horse. Remembering this, I felt sad.

The tram rolled and pitched, its warning bell ringing all the time. A man stumbled up and down the aisle, all but falling over as he dispensed tickets with some kind of machine that made a cranking and punching sound.

The tram suddenly stopped, and I was almost hurled out of my seat.

The ticket man shouted "Dadar Center!" and Mr. Ras Mohun caught my hand. I followed him out of the tram.

In Dadar Center, Mr. Ras Mohun bought me a pair of shoes with laces. My feet had grown, and my old shoes with the buckles were too tight for me.

❦

ONE AFTERNOON when I ran into the sitting-and-dining room for tiffin, Mr. Ras Mohun called out, "Stop! Whenever you come in, you must say, 'Good afternoon, Uncle. Good afternoon, Auntie'—or, if it is the morning, 'Good morning, Uncle. Good morning, Auntie.' "

"Good afternoon, Uncle. Good afternoon, Auntie," I said, plunking myself into my chair.

"No, not that way," Mrs. Ras Mohun said. "Only jungly boys sit down like that. Stand up."

I stood up.

"Another thing," Mrs. Ras Mohun continued. "If we ask you, when you come in, 'How are you?' you should say 'I'm quite well and happy, thank you'—and say it with a good smile—before sitting down."

"You're fortunate in having a naturally good smile," Mr. Ras Mohun said.

"But sometimes he looks sad," Mrs. Ras Mohun said.

"That's natural," Mr. Ras Mohun said. "He's homesick for the Punjab."

"Let's hear you say, 'I'm quite well and happy, thank you,' with a good smile," Mrs. Ras Mohun said.

"I'm quite well and happy, thank you," I said as rapidly as I could, trying to smile without being quite sure what a good smile looked like.

"Just wrinkle your nose a little less," Mr. Ras Mohun said.

He got up and came to me. I thought he was going to fix the wrinkles on my nose, but he bent down, slipped his hands between my feet, and pulled them apart, this time making my toes point out.

"That's right," he said. "Stand just as you are. Now put your hands behind your back and clasp them—just your fingers. That's right. Now you are standing at ease. This is how you stand when you're waiting for Auntie and me to return your greeting. In fact, whenever you are talking to me or Auntie anywhere in the school, you can stand at ease. But when you come to my office to see me, then you should stand at attention."

He slapped my feet together, making me almost lose my balance. I steadied myself by catching hold of his short hair.

"No, no, drop your hands to your sides," he said. "When you stand at attention, your hands should always be at your sides."

Afterward, I never entered the sitting-and-dining

room without stopping at the door, separating my feet a few inches, with my toes out, putting my hands at my back, and exchanging cheerful greetings with Mr. and Mrs. Ras Mohun. (It was years before I learned that if someone asked "How are you?" I could say "I don't feel well." Also, I never talked to any superior without automatically bringing my feet together and dropping my hands to my sides—except when I was bothered by an itch or a fly. Then I was likely to forget Mr. Ras Mohun's lesson.)

IV

PLAYMATE

"I WANT A ROCKING HORSE AND A MOUTH ORGAN AND a Meccano set," I said to Mr. and Mrs. Ras Mohun at dinner.

"Are those the toys you had at home?" Mr. Ras Mohun asked me.

I had to think for a moment—sometimes everything connected with home seemed so far away. "Yes," I said.

"And you miss them?" Mr. Ras Mohun asked.

"I want them," I said. "Now, Uncle."

"You should try to make your own toys," Mrs Ras Mohun said.

"All good children make their own toys," Mr. Ras Mohun said.

After dinner, before I went back to the boys' dormitory, Mr. Ras Mohun gave me two empty cylindrical cigarette tins to play with. At first, I didn't know what to do with them, but then I got an idea. I made a hole with a nail in the bottom of each cigarette tin and linked them with a long string. I gave one cigarette tin to Deoji and ran with the other as far as I could go. I shouted into my cigarette tin, "Hello, hello! This is me at this end! Who is that speaking?"

I held the cigarette tin so close against my mouth that I was almost unable to hear myself speak.

I then put the cigarette tin to my ear and tried to catch what Deoji was saying into his cigarette tin. All I ever heard was a hum, but I liked the game.

I tired of the telephone game within a few days,

and got another idea, after Mr. Ras Mohun described to me how he had sent a telegram to Daddyji saying that I was doing well. "I gave the message to the postal clerk," Mr. Ras Mohun said. "He sent it out on the machine—tap-tap-tap-tap, tap, tap, tap-tap. The message must have got to the Punjab almost immediately."

That day, I took the drawer of an ordinary wooden matchbox, about two inches long, wrapped a thread around its middle many times over, inserted a matchstick through the bunched-up thread on the top, and slid the matchstick up and down so that I could turn it round and round in the box until the thread became very taut and the matchstick stood almost upright against the bottom of the drawer. I held the drawer in one hand and flicked the matchstick rapidly with the fingers of the other and listened excitedly to the clatter of wood against wood: "Tap-tap-tap-tap, tap, tap, tap-tap." I pretended I was sending a telegram home: "NEED MOUTH ORGAN HORSE MECCANO SET PLEASE SEND."

Soon the other boys acquired their own match-drawer machines, and although Mr. Ras Mohun forbade their use outside the boys' dormitory we were free to play with them as we liked within its precincts. We would hold clattering races lasting for hours, to see who could flick his matchstick the fastest and make the most din.

THE RAIN CAME down in big streams. Abdul said the gods had opened all their pipes—and their pipes had big mouths and strong water pressure. The rain would stop only to start again.

In the back courtyard, the wet grass came up almost to my knees. When the rain stopped, several of us boys slipped out and lay in the wet grass—with every part of us covered—and pretended we were animals.

"The rains bring out the snakes," Abdul said. He was eleven and was totally blind. "There is a boa constrictor who lives up in that tree just beyond this courtyard—you know, the tree where the shrieking vultures nest. The boa has been known to drop down and kill a blind boy by wrapping himself around him. If the boa gets you, you will hear him hiss and feel him sway his head in enjoyment as he crushes your bones and listens to your ribs crack and snap. He will then climb up the tree again and leave the corpse in the grass for another blind boy to stumble over."

"I'll get a pocket knife and cut him up if he comes near me," I said.

"If you cut a boa constrictor, you get two snakes instead of one," Abdul said. "And if you cut it twice, you get three snakes. They multiply. And a cut boa constrictor is much more dangerous. He coils himself and flies noiselessly through the air and kills by biting on the forehead or on the cheek. A sighted person will see him coming and run and hide, but a blind person won't know. Most blind people die of such snake bites."

I clung to his arm.

The next morning, I wouldn't get out from under my mosquito net.

"What's the matter?" Deoji asked.

"Snakes!" I cried. "I need a snake net!" I told him about the boa constrictor in the tree.

"True, there are snakes here that fly and multiply," Deoji said. "But during the day they live underground, and they only come out in the night. Abdul is just trying to frighten you. He would frighten Mr. Ras Mohun if he could. He is an uncontrollable mischief-maker."

After that, I looked for ways to frighten Abdul.

One day, I knotted a piece of string into a series of continuous loops, so that it felt like a strip of little bumps and depressions. I coiled the string with an end sticking out, made my hand into the shape of a basket, and put the coil in it. I went to Abdul. "Feel what I have in my hand, Abdul," I said, tugging at his hand.

"First tell me what it is," Abdul said, drawing back.

"Well, if you don't want to feel I won't tell you."

Abdul grew curious.

I held my cupped hand out to him. He cautiously reached out and touched the string.

"Watch out! It's a snake!" I cried.

"Snake in the boys' dormitory!" Addul cried out, and he ran for the door.

I laughed, and he realized that he had been taken in. He grabbed my arm and twisted it until I thought he would break it. He was twice my height and very tough.

I begged for my life and promised never to play a trick on him again. He let me go.

When I was sure that Abdul had forgotten the incident, I knotted another, much longer piece of string and put a little bit of Lifebuoy soap on it to make it slithery. Then, in the back courtyard, I threw it, lasso fashion, around Abdul's neck and hissed, swaying my head.

"Watch it—it's the boa constrictor!"

He screamed with fright, but he quickly realized that he had been taken in once again. He caught hold of me, but this time I was prepared for him, and I was able to struggle free and run away.

Later that day, after his dinner, Abdul bounded up the stairs. "And what did you eat today!" he asked, trying to catch me.

"Mutton on toast," I said. "Mutton is Uncle and Auntie's very favorite food, but we only have it once a week."

He sniffed. "Nothing like good thick maize bread with lentils and spinach to build up one's strength," he said, and he made some snide remarks about my soft diet, my soft bed, my soft clothes—my sissy privileges.

"You're a dirty street boy," I said. "You're a common beggar."

We all knew that before coming to the school Abdul had been a street boy who lived by begging. He had tried to snatch the handbag of a passerby who stopped to give him money, and the police had picked him up and taken him to a home for delinquents. The wardens there hadn't known what to do with a totally blind delinquent, and had brought him to Mr. Ras Mohun, who had agreed to give him an opportunity at his school.

Abdul now caught hold of me and held my hands in a tight grip. "Soft and ladylike!" he taunted. "Toast and mutton! Soft and ladylike!" Abdul's rough hands

were marked with scabs and smelled of tobacco. He
caned chairs in the school's workshop and smoked on
the sly.

I didn't like my special privileges, but neither did I
like Abdul, who was constantly ridiculing me for them
in front of the other boys.

I yanked my hands free and ran down the boys'
staircase, weaving from one side of the steps to the other
to elude him, while he followed close behind, his
leathery feet slapping on the stairs. Downstairs, I headed
straight for the workshop and quickly found the chair
he usually squatted by and caned. Only part of the seat
was finished, with a pattern of holes; the rest of the
frame was taut bands of cane. On the seat was a caning
knife. I picked it up and, without knowing exactly what
I was doing, slashed some of the bands.

He heard and knew.

I jumped over the chair and hid behind a work-
table while Abdul crashed around the workshop, stumbling over chairs and cursing. "Wait till I find you!" he
cried. "I'll cut off your ladylike hands!"

Abdul's best friend, Tarak Nath, came running into
the workshop to see what was happening. He was partially sighted, and, like the few other partially sighted
boys in the school, was much in demand as a friend by
totally blind boys. I feared that he would deliver me to
Abdul, but he stuck to the rules of fair play—that a
partially sighted boy should not interfere in a quarrel
between totally blind boys.

Abdul was almost upon me. I dashed from under
the table and ran up to the boys' dormitory and to

Deoji. For days afterward, I had to be careful not to be caught alone by Abdul.

Then, one day, I got some money from home. I gave half of it to Abdul to repay him for his extra work on the chair and to make up with him.

"If I promise to let you in on a new boys'-dormitory secret, will you give me the rest of your money?" he asked.

At first, I refused, but then I couldn't contain my curiosity and I gave him the money.

That night, when we were in our beds, Abdul came and got me. I followed him out of the boys' dormitory, thinking that we were going to the boys' common bathroom—most of us were afraid to go there alone. But he turned down the boys' staircase. I wanted to go back, remembering that snakes and ghosts came out at night, but my curiosity was aroused, and I continued to follow him. He walked across the veranda, toward the school gate. I was afraid that he meant to run away and become a street beggar again, taking me with him. I stopped. He caught hold of me and dragged me toward the wall that the school shared with the Tata Mill. He put my hands on some bars in the wall. They were rusty and felt like a dirty old horseshoe I had played with at home.

"What is this?" I asked.

"It's the bars of a window of the Muhammadan Hotel, where the mill hands go."

Abdul tapped on the window glass behind the bars with an anna. The clink of the coin on the glass sounded loud in the night air. I was sure that we would be discovered by Mr. Ras Mohun and punished with the ruler.

Abruptly, the window was opened from the other side of the bars, and a voice said softly, "Rosewater, lemon drops, *bhel-puri.*" *Bhel-puri,* hot and spicy snacks, are street foods of Bombay.

"Everything for the two of us," Abdul said, handing in some money.

Someone handed us through the bars two bottles of rose drink, two bags of lemon drops, and two paper cones of *bhel-puri.*

"Quick, eat and drink," Abdul said to me. "We have to return the bottles."

I had never had *bhel-puri* before, and they set my mouth on fire, but the lemon drops sweetened my mouth and the rosewater cooled it. I thought I had never tasted a better combination of delights. As we were returning upstairs, I asked Abdul in a whisper why we had to go the the Muhammadan Hotel like thieves in the night.

"Mr. Ras Mohun is a clean Christian, and the Muhammadan Hotel is run by a dirty Muslim," he said. "I am a Muslim. I like dirty Muslim food."

"When I finish being a Hindu, I will become a Muslim, and then I'll eat only your Muslim food," I said.

Following that night, Abdul and I and some friends of ours who were in on the secret would slip downstairs after bedtime whenever any of us had any money; the boys used to receive money for caning chairs, or from their missionary mummies and daddies, and I used to receive a little pocket money from home. We would tap on the bars of the Muhammadan Hotel and eat and drink. I remember that once the Muhammadan Hotel introduced a new treat—a sweet that had the feel of cotton and the taste of powdered sugar. The sweet immediately became our favorite, and Abdul named it "mother's kisses."

V

BELL

"Wake up, Vedi!" Deoji would say, gently pulling my cheek with his small, cold hand. "It's six o'clock."

I would remember Daddyji's warm and enveloping hand on my forehead in the morning, and I would feel sad. Daddyji used to make many trips into my room to wake me, but each time he tiptoed away. Finally, as he was leaving for the office, he laid his hand on my forehead—so lightly that it seemed to be a hand in a dream—and I woke up.

"Wake up," Deoji would say, his hand pulling my cheek. "Mr. Ras Mohun has rung the wake-up bell."

Mr. Ras Mohun, who was the only person in the school with a watch, was in charge of the bell. Whatever he was doing—looking after Heea upstairs or working in his office downstairs or teaching us or supervising us—he never forgot to ring the bell at the appointed times, and wherever we were in the school we heard him.

"Let me sleep," I would beg Deoji, pulling the bedclothes over my head. "I want to finish my dream."

"The Sighted Master will report you to Mr. Ras Mohun," he would say. "That's the Sighted Master's duty."

I would get down from my bed and quickly wash and dress, just in time to join the hymn line in the boys' dormitory when Mr. Ras Mohun rang the hymn bell. With the Sighted Master prompting us, we would sing in Marathi a few Christian songs, like "When the Saints Go Marching In," that Mr. Ras Mohun had taught us, and we would sing almost in a shout, so that he, in the tower upstairs, and Jesus, Mary, and Joseph, sitting above him, would hear us and give us merit points. Sometimes we would hear the girls shouting from their side, and we would shout louder. I liked to sing the hymns, although Deoji once told me, "I have heard these hymns sung in English a few times, in the church of my missionary mummy and daddy, and they sound very different. There, when you sing 'When the Saints Go Marching In,' you think angels are lifting you up. But here, when we sing them in Marathi, I feel we are a chorus of frogs singing to the bathroom ghost. What a pity that is!"

Sometimes we would hear Mr. Ras Mohun's breakfast bell when we were in the middle of a hymn, and the other boys would rush downstairs to the veranda for their breakfast, while I would run into the sitting-and-dining room for mine. At my separate table, I was usually served porridge, toast, and, occasionally, a soft-boiled egg, which I had learned to eat with a spoon without getting egg all over my bib.

The boys would come back from their breakfast smelling of coconut and groundnuts and spinach—all delicious things that I couldn't have. We would all set about cleaning the boys' dormitory—making our beds and tidying up our boxes, under the supervision of the Sighted Master. At the sound of the class bell, we would go down for our morning class.

The morning class was held in the school's only

classroom. I remember that we sat on straight-backed, cane-bottomed, armless chairs—only the teacher's chair had arms—at long tables and studied birds and animals with the pupil-teacher, Miss Mary. I also remember that Miss Mary was partially sighted, was fourteen years old, and had come to the school when she was as small as I was. She had studied up through the fourth standard—as far as the school went. Then she had had nothing to do and nowhere to go, so Mr. Ras Mohun had hired her as a pupil-teacher. At the time he hired her, she was twelve.

I didn't like sitting in a chair. I didn't know what to do with my legs. Every time I moved my legs, they made a noise, and then Miss Mary would tell me to sit quietly, like a good boy. Also, in the class we boys had to sit on one side and the girls on the other. I often wanted to jump across to the girls' side and sit with Paran. But Abdul told me, "Girl-mischief of that kind, if Mr. Ras Mohun comes to know of it, is worth two raps on the knuckles and two swats on the behind with the ruler, and Mr. Ras Mohun's ruler is not your ordinary ruler—thin and flat—but thick and round, like a policeman's swagger stick."

Once, I remember, Miss Mary handed me something fluffy and bulgy and made out of cloth. "What is it, Vedi?" she asked.

"A stuffed bird," I said absently. I didn't feel it carefully, because I was thinking about the touch of Miss Mary's hands—how they were as gentle and slightly moist as Abdul's were rough and dry—and about how sweetly she spoke Marathi.

Everyone laughed.

"Of course, it's a stuffed bird, silly, but what is it called?" Abdul put in.

Miss Mary took it from me and gave it to Reuben, who was sitting next to me. He was eleven and was totally blind. "What is it, Reuben?" she asked.

"A dove, Miss Mary."

I heard Miss Mary's bare feet slap across to Paran's chair. "What is it, Paran?"

"Reuben is wrong," Paran said. "It's not a dove at all. It's a quail."

I heard Miss Mary walk across to Bhaskar's chair. Bhaskar was nine and was half sighted.

"No, Miss Mary, they're all wrong," he said. "It's a pigeon."

She came back to my chair and put the stuffed thing in front of me. "Try again, Vedi," she said. "Can you tell what kind of bird it is?"

"I want to go outside and play," I said, without touching the stuffed thing.

"But you're in a class now," Miss Mary said. "What kind of bird is it, Vedi?"

I picked up the soft, round thing and felt it all over. It had a beak, claws, and a tail.

"It's a myna."

Everybody laughed.

"What's a myna? There is no such thing," Abdul said.

"It's a talking bird."

Everybody laughed again.

"Birds don't talk," Abdul said. "You're the son of an owl."

"Abdul, don't be abusive," Miss Mary said. (In India, the owl is considered to be foolish.)

"If Vedi weren't so small, he would know better," Deoji said.

"Our servant Sher Singh told me about a myna he knew," I said. "She was a bird and she would sit on his shoulder and talk."

"You're a good storyteller," Abdul said.

Miss Mary shushed them. "I think Mr. Ras Mohun taught me that there is a bird in the Punjab that can say a few words, but I'm not sure what it's called. Anyway, you're all wrong. This is a sparrow."

She handed some other stuffed things around, talking all the time. "This is a dove. It's a little bigger than a sparrow. . . . This is a pigeon. It's fatter than the dove. . . . This is a toy buffalo. You feel these horns? . . . This is a toy monkey. He has long arms, which he uses to swing from tree to tree. . . . This is a toy elephant. You can always tell an elephant by its trunk in the front."

"I want to see a real elephant," I said.

"Blind people can never see a real elephant," Miss Mary said. "But if sighted people say to you, 'There goes an elephant,' you should know what they mean."

I wanted to argue the matter with her, but just then we heard the lunch bell.

After lunch, Mr. Ras Mohun would ring the Braille-class bell, for our Braille lesson with the Matron.

I didn't know much about the Matron except that she was the "Sighted Master" of the girls' dormitory—that she slept there and kept order there. I'd never heard the word "matron" before and was struck by its resem-

blance to "train;" for months I imagined that the Matron had arrived at the school on a train when she was
as small as I was, and, like Miss Mary, had stayed on
because she had nowhere else to go.

One day, in the Braille class, the Matron set in front
of me a wooden slate a little larger than an ordinary
sheet of paper, with a couple of nails and a small hinged
plate at the top. It had a recessed track of small round
holes a couple of inches apart along each side. She
leaned over the table from behind me. She had a big
stomach, which hung out over her sari, and because she
had very short arms it seemed even bigger. Her stomach
was damp with sweat, and she smelled of onions and
betel nuts.

I tried to slip out from under her, but she caught
hold of my hand and began to show me how to align
a cardboardlike piece of special Braille paper in the middle of the slate, hook it on the two nails at the top, and
lock it in place with the hinged plate. She then handed
me something called a guide. It was two metal strips a
couple of inches high and a little wider than the slate,
connected at one side by a hinge, with two pegs behind
the back strip. The Matron took my forefinger and ran
it along the front strip of the guide, pointing out two
rows of about thirty little openings, each of which just
fitted the tip of my forefinger. She then pointed out on
the back strip two corresponding rows of little hollowed-
out dots in identical groups of six, and told me that each
group was called a cell. She showed me how, when the
guide was closed and the two strips lay on each other,
each opening served as a sort of frame for a cell. She

showed me how to slip the back strip under the paper from the left side, fit the pegs into the two top holes of the tracks, and then close the guide, so that the paper was clamped between the two strips.

She then handed me something called a stylus—a small wooden knob with a steel pin on it. She showed me how to hold the stylus in my hand, with the knob in the crook of my right forefinger so that the steel pin was pointing down, and how to punch dots in the paper through the openings in the guide, from the right, using my left forefinger to help direct the pin of the stylus in each cell.

"You're now ready to write the first two lines of Braille on your paper," she said. "But remember that you're punching dots from the back—that Braille is written backward. Different patterns of dots in a cell stand for different English letters. When you have filled two rows of cells with any groups of dots you like, move the guide down to the next holes on the slate, and then you can write two more lines." She had a deep voice and breathed heavily, but she spoke Marathi sweetly, like Miss Mary.

The Matron moved on, and I tried to punch my first line of Braille dots. The head of the stylus was too big for the crook of my finger. So much pressure was required to punch a dot through the thick paper that I had to climb on the chair, hold the stylus with both hands, and press it down with all my weight. When I tried to write in this way, the slate, which was so long that it stuck out over the edge of the table, jabbed me in the stomach. Since my left hand was busy pressing down on the stylus, I couldn't help direct the pin of the stylus, so I couldn't tell what dots I was punching in each cell.

I took the paper out of the guide and out of the hinged plate and turned it over, Braille side up. I touched the Braille dots I had made; each dot was sharp and distinct—not torn and obscure, as when I put a pin through a piece of paper. But I realized I had no idea what the dots meant. Then I heard the Matron exclaim, "There, Vedi! You're reading now!"

I felt excited, and remembered sitting on my rocking horse and rocking away, and playing all the notes on my mouth organ, from one end to the other, and making my first motorcar out of my Meccano set.

"Children who don't know yet how to write Braille," the Matron was saying to the class, "take the paper out of your guide, run your forefinger first down the left side of the first cell of the guide, and then down the right side, and count off with me, from top to bottom, 'Dot one, dot two, dot three—dot four, dot five, dot six.' These six dots, in various combinations, stand for all the English Braille letters. But not all the possible combinations of dots are used up by the twenty-six letters of the English alphabet. So some of these dots and combinations are used for English punctuation marks; dot six before any letter stands for a capital. Other combinations of dots are English contraction signs for everyday words like 'and,' 'for,' 'of.' "

She turned to me. "Can you tell me now, Vedi, what a contraction is?"

"I don't understand anything," I said.

She explained again and repeated her question.

"Contractions are little words like 'and,' 'for,' and 'of,' " I said, repeating what I thought she had said.

"Good boy," she said, patting me on the back. "Now see if you can write some more."

I tried to realign my Braille paper in the slate. The old holes in the paper where it had originally hooked on to the nails under the hinged plate tore, and the paper shifted in the guide. Consequently, the new dots I made went in a crooked line and ran into dots I had made earlier, jumbling everything.

All around me was the clatter of wood, metal, and paper—of Braille dots being punched in the thick paper, of steel pins clicking along the cells of the guides, of guides being shifted down the slate tracks, of hinged plates being opened and snapped shut. Ahead, there was the tick-tick-tick-tick of Deoji (fast, like the pitter-patter of my baby sister Usha's feet); from the left, there was the tick, tick, tick, tick of Bhaskar (lumbering, like the swish-and-jerk of strips of cane being drawn through the chair frames); from the right, there was the tick-tick, tick-tick of Abdul (sudden, like the click-click of Mr. Ras Mohun's shoes).

I remembered the quiet scratchings of my sister Umi's pencil running along in her copybook and the delicate strokes of my sister Pom's fountain pen flowing along her pad. I remembered the soothing, almost imperceptible sound of Sister Umi turning a page of her copybook and the cozy, rippling sound of Sister Pom tearing a page out of her pad.

"Matron!" I cried out. "I want pencil and paper! I want to write like Sister Umi."

"Bhaskar is half sighted, and even he can't write

with pencil and paper," the Matron said. "What makes you think that you can?"

"I want pencil and paper!" I shouted, and I flung the guide down on the floor. I would have flung the slate after it except that it was too large and heavy.

"Think of your Braille slate and guide as a new toy," the Matron said, picking up the guide and giving it to me. "You can write a secret message to Abdul."

That idea kept me at my Braille slate for a while, but I soon grew tired of it. I let the stylus drop on the table and sat scratching my legs.

In time—I don't know how many days or weeks or months it was—my stylus finger grew, my hand grew, my strength grew, and I learned to align the paper on the slate properly and write Braille correctly. I remember that in order to memorize which dots stood for which letters I would think of combinations of dots as telephone numbers, and of the letters formed by the combinations as standing for members of my family. When I punched (or dialled) one, three, six, I got "u," for Umi; when I punched one, two, three, four, I got "p," for Pom; when I punched one, three, four, I got "m," for Mamaji. The Braille letters would race through my fingers into the stylus, along the guide, and down the slate, filling the paper with simple English words, like "cat," "mat," and "sat."

We always knew when the Braille class was over because Mr. Ras Mohun would come into the room ringing the bell. The Matron would leave, and Mr. Ras Mohun himself would start teaching. His subject was Bible stories and general knowledge. It was the only class for which we had a book—a copy for each of us.

The book, which was in English, was called "Bible Stories for Boys and Girls." It had a smooth, hard cover, and every time I touched it I thought of a tall marble statue of a mother and child which stood on the mantelpiece in our drawing room at home.

"A good Bible reader is a good Braille reader," Mr. Ras Mohun would say. "And a good Braille reader sits properly. A bad Braille reader reads with the tip of only a forefinger, but a good Braille reader reads with the tips of all eight fingers—with both hands. He doesn't press down hard on the letters. He doesn't move his lips or whisper to himself when he's reading. He keeps his arms straight. He bends his hands slightly, so that his fingers are at an angle to the book. He keeps his book level on the desk."

I paid attention to Mr. Ras Mohun's directions and learned to read "Bible Stories" quickly. Each letter of the book fitted easily under the tip of a finger—the book was embossed without any contraction signs, and there were wide spaces between the lines—and I liked the feel of a line of well-embossed Braille letters. Abdul could read with only his right forefinger, but from the very start I practiced reading like Deoji, with all eight fingers. I used to imagine that each of my fingers was a student—Abdul, Deoji, Bhaskar, Paran—and that they were all competing to see which one of them could read the fastest. The left little finger was the laggard, like Abdul. The right forefinger was the star, like Deoji. To bring the laggard finger up to the level of the star finger, I would practice reading with only the left little finger. But it seemed that, try as I might, there was no way to make the laggard catch up.

"I am determined to become a good Braille reader, even faster than Deoji, so that I can become a doctor, like Daddyji," I said to Abdul one day.

"I would rather be a carpenter than a doctor," Abdul said, referring to a story in the book. In the story, Jesus said that being a carpenter was just as good as being a doctor. Abdul took special delight in the idea because "carpentry and caning are like chair and seat— they go together," he said. "I'd rather cane chairs than read stupid Braille."

Sometimes when I was reading Braille, my hands would get cold, and I would sit on them and wonder if I could ever learn to read Braille with my chin.

Mr. Ras Mohun would conclude the Bible-stories-and-general-knowledge class by ringing the bell from wherever he happened to be standing. Many boys and girls would thereupon go to the veranda for the music class, which was taught by another pupil-teacher, Mr. Joseph, or to the workshop, in the back part of the classroom, to cane chairs under the direction of the Sighted Master.

I wanted to go to the music class, because Deoji went there, and to the caning class, because Abdul went there. I remember that nice sounds of stringed instruments came from the music class, and that once Abdul came upstairs to the boys' dormitory from caning and announced, to great general excitement, that the caning class had received an order to make shirt buttons out of coconut shells.

"I want to make shirt buttons with you," I said.

"Mr. Ras Mohun won't let you," Abdul said.

"Yes, he will."

When I told Mr. Ras Mohun about what I was going to do, he said, "You are not to go to either the workshop or the music class. Your father has forbidden it. Children who cane chairs or play stringed instruments get calluses on their fingers, and then they can't read Braille well. And your father has high hopes for you."

I didn't know exactly what calluses were until Deoji let me feel his fingers after he had started learning to play the *dilrubah* in music class. They had got swollen and hard. "In music class here, we only have cheap instruments with sharp strings, like the *dilrubah,* which is good for street music," Deoji told me. "I am praying to Jesus, Mary, and Joseph that when I grow up I will have a violin, which is played in the drawing rooms of well-to-do homes. It has nice strings and doesn't require too much pressure from the fingers."

As it happened, the shirt-button order was cancelled, because the job proved too difficult for the caning class, but before it was cancelled the workshop acquired a metal bench vise. I remember that I used to slip down to the workshop in the evening and play with it secretly. I would put my fingers between its serrated lips and turn the handle bit by bit to see how much pressure my fingers could stand—all the time hoping that I would get calluses, like Deoji's. I never did, although sometimes I had trouble extricating my fingers, and afterward I would carry the impressions of the serrated lips for a few minutes.

Following Mr. Ras Mohun's class, when everyone else went to the music class or the workshop, I would go down into the cellar and play with Miss Mary. In the cellar, Miss Mary once showed me several heavy wooden bars with wooden balls at the ends. "These are dumbbells," she said. "When you grow big, you will be able to lift them and grow bigger."

She picked me up and showed me metal rings hanging from the ceiling.

I caught hold of the rings and slipped out of her arms and swung like a monkey. "Catch me!" I called out to her, and I swung fast and high until I was giddy. I jumped down and shouted, "Again, Miss Mary!"

Just then, Mr. Ras Mohun rang the tiffin bell, and I ran upstairs to the sitting-and-dining room.

I would swallow my tiffin—a cup of hot milk with soggy pieces of bread in it—as quickly as I could and race down to the back courtyard, where everyone would be waiting for Mr. Ras Mohun to ring the game bell. The back courtyard was so small that if Abdul, Deoji, and I had joined hands, extended our arms, and swung around, we could almost have touched all four walls, but into it a seesaw, a swing, and a combination of climbing bars and a slide had somehow been fitted. During the game period, the Sighted Master and the Matron would see to it that we all got a turn on one or another of these.

After the game period, there would be the relaxing bell, and we boys would all go to the boys' dormitory and sit on our beds and talk. Now and again, Mrs. Ras Mohun would come and get two or three of us and give us a gardening lesson at a patch along one wall of the back courtyard, known as Mrs. Ras Mohun's flower-and-vegetable bed.

I remember that one time we planted a couple of

rosebushes, and every morning we went down to feel them. Abdul couldn't understand why the rosebushes had thorns. Bhaskar said that it was because ghosts liked the smell of roses and didn't want us to pick them. Another time, we planted some potatoes, and I couldn't understand why they grew underground. Bhaskar said that it was because ghosts lived underground and liked to eat potatoes.

After the relaxing period, there were two other bells—the dinner bell and the sleep bell.

I remember that once, after the sleep bell, Mr. Ras Mohun caught me out of my bed, and summoned me to his office the next morning.

"Yes? Speak, Vedi, speak," he said. "You have made me very unhappy by being out of your bed after the sleep bell." He tapped what I was sure was his ruler on his desk impatiently, as if his hand were twitching to beat me.

I couldn't find my voice, even though he kept on urging me to speak. I thought what a funny way he had of speaking. He said "yetsh" and "shpeak" and "unhoppy." (He had the same funny way of speaking Marathi; I later learned that the accent was characteristic of many Bengalis.) Yet when he addressed me by name I would start, for it seemed that Mamaji was calling me. Many women's voices were not as high-pitched as his. I remember that he had a thin falsetto voice, which was always pitched on more or less the same note and had a weary quality. Perhaps because he was angry now, his voice was cracking, like Mamaji's. (She had long suffered from asthma, which had clouded her voice, but she had a much greater range of tones than

Mr. Ras Mohun did.) I found myself listening to Mr. Ras Mohun's voice and trying to remember Mamaji's voice.

"Shpeak, boy, shpeak."

I jumped. "I was in the boys' common bathroom and couldn't get quickly into my bell—I mean, my bed, Uncle."

SATURDAYS AND SUNDAYS, the boys ordinarily had to stay in the boys' dormitory and the girls in the girls' dormitory. But now and then the Sighted Master and the Matron would organize outings or games for us.

Sometimes we went on outings to Mahim Sea Beach. Those of us who were totally blind walked with the partially sighted, in twos or threes, but boys could walk only with boys, and girls only with girls. Mahim Sea Beach was far away, beyond Dadar Pool and Shivaji Park. Because I was small, I had trouble keeping up with the others, and quickly got tired. Sometimes I would sit down on the way and ask to be carried. If I was walking with Bhaskar and Deoji, Bhaskar would get angry and go ahead, but Deoji would stay back with me. Sometimes Deoji and I would reach Mahim Sea Beach only as the others were starting back. Mahim Sea Beach smelled like the boys' common bathroom, the mud underfoot was slippery, and the water was so shallow that I had to sit down even to get my legs wet. Just the same, we always felt refreshed after the outing.

One Saturday, Abdul announced in the boys' dormitory, "The Sighted Master has found a new game for us."

All of us gathered around Abdul to find out what it was.

"It has to do with a long rope," he said.

"They are going to hang Jaisingh, so that the rest of us can sleep," Tarak Nath said.

Everyone laughed at Tarak Nath's remark. None of us liked the deaf, dumb, and blind Jaisingh much, because he cried in the middle of the night for no reason at all; in fact, we scorned him, as we imagined that the sighted scorned all of us.

Bhaskar wanted to know if this was the game he had been dreaming about, in which boys and girls could play together and touch each other.

"No," Abdul said. "There are no such games for the blind. As long as Mr. Ras Mohun has his ruler, such games will not be played here."

We all cursed Abdul for never letting us forget Mr. Ras Mohun's ruler.

That afternoon, the Sighted Master called us all to the postage stamp of a front courtyard for the game. He let us feel a huge rope that was coiled up on the ground. It was rough and abrasive and muddy and so thick that my hands could scarcely go round it. Following the Sighted Master's directions, we uncoiled the rope and laid it out on the ground, organized ourselves into two parties, dug a line across the middle of the muddy courtyard, and took places along the rope, on either side of the line. We held the rope up, nestling it under our arms. The Sighted Master shouted "Go!" and we started pulling. Deoji was very strong and he was on my side of the line, and our team pulled everyone on the other across the line. All of us liked the game very much, because at the end we all fell on each other in a heap in the mud. We begged to play some more, but the Sighted Master said, "This is a tug-of-war. Mr. Ras Mohun says you can hurt yourself, so it must be played only once in a while, under my supervision." It was many weeks before we got a chance to have a tug-of-war again.

V I

BLACKWATER
ISLAND

"THE WORST THING A PERSON CAN DO TO BLIND children is to coddle them," Mr. Ras Mohun used to say to Mrs. Ras Mohun. "Activities and hard knocks are the best thing for their development. Vedi's lucky that he's so naturally active."

I never walked anywhere but always ran, not caring what was in the way. Sometimes I would forget where a wall or a post was, and would crash into it. Other times, a bed or a chair would have been moved, or a door left half open—generally by a partially sighted person—and I would run into it. There was hardly a day when I did not get a cut or a bump, and the cuts and bumps were most often on the forehead, the eyebrows, or the shins. Once, my shins would not stop bleeding, even after Mrs. Ras Mohun repeatedly applied tincture of iodine to them. She had to bandage my legs from knee to ankle. The bandages stayed on for several days, and after Mrs. Ras Mohun took them off I was careful for a while. When I injured the same area again and again, it became so tender that sometimes a proper scab would not form, and a mere bit of friction in bed would start up the bleeding again. I did not give the cuts and bruises much thought, but I automatically learned to sleep on my side in such a manner that they would not touch the sheets or the pillow.

All of us totally blind boys were constantly hitting ourselves against something or other. We would feel each other's bumps and injuries, and we would joke about them. "Let me feel," we would say. "Is it on your

hood or on your mudguard? Or is it the wheel again?"
"Hood" was our slang for a forehead, "mudguard" for
an eyebrow, and "wheel" for a shin. We had special
names for bumps on special spots—like "horns" for
bumps on the sides of the forehead. "Have you got one
horn on your hood or two?" we might say. "Oh, that's
a big horn!" Even as we made light of our injuries, we
endowed whatever we hit—or whatever hit us, as we
came to think of it—with the malevolence we attributed
to the entire sighted world. It seemed to us that a sta-
tionary object, like a wall, no less than a familiar object
in an unfamiliar place, like a chair that had been
moved, would willfully loom out of the sighted world
to vex us. Whenever we hurt ourselves on anything at
all, we would kick it and beat it and cry out, "The
sighted bastards!" And yet sometimes our injuries came
not from the sighted world but from our own careless-
ness.

One day, Abdul and Bhaskar were on the swing in
the back courtyard. I could feel the whoosh of air as the
swing repeatedly flew past my head—first coming, then
going back. The swing board was held on the rope only
by a notch in each end. When the swingers went too
high, the board would sometimes come unhooked from
the rope and spill them. I feared that Abdul and Bhaskar would get thrown and hurt themselves. Besides, it
was long past time for me to have my turn on the
swing. "Stop!" I shouted. "It's my turn!" Instead of
stopping, Abdul and Bhaskar pumped the swing harder
and faster and higher, as if they were a couple of
trapped birds trying to escape from the courtyard. Now

the swing was way up here, now way back there, coming and going so fast that I was aware only of one whoosh of air after another sweeping by my head. "Catch us and you can have the swing!" Bhaskar shouted breathlessly, his voice ricocheting in the well of the back courtyard.

When the swingers did not play fair, we would often stop the swing by rushing at the rope from the front, catching hold of it, and dragging our feet along the ground. We might be carried aloft by the momentum for a few swings, but eventually the swing would come to a stop. I listened carefully to the whooshes of air, and when I was sure that the swing was just in front of me I dashed forward with my arms outstretched. But I had forgotten momentarily that Bhaskar had one good eye and could see me coming. I heard the board squeak against the rope as the swing was jerked to the side out of my reach. Suddenly, the rope wasn't where I had expected it to be, and I remember thinking that I was going to fall. But the swing, it turned out, was going so fast that Bhaskar wasn't able to jerk it far enough, and a corner of the board struck me like a hammer blow in the middle of my forehead. I staggered and fainted.

When I woke up, I had the odd sensation that my forehead was frozen and that someone was scratching it with the point of an icepick—the kind that the servants used at home to break a block of ice for the ice chest.

"Don't!" I cried, trying to wriggle out from under it.

"Lie still," said a strange man's voice that seemed

to be coming from above my head. "I'm stitching up your wound. It's really a bad one. You're lucky that your brain was spared."

I began to cry.

"You're just in pain. Try to go to sleep," the man said, and he tied a bandage around my head so tightly that it seemed to bunch up the skin on my forehead under it.

I remember that I slept; that I had to sleep on my back, because every time I turned on my side in my sleep I felt that the man was jabbing my forehead with the icepick again; and that I didn't wake up for a long time. I remember that the moment I woke up I examined the wound through the bandage. It felt as if someone had branded me. I had heard that really bad criminals were permanently branded on their foreheads with an iron and abandoned on Blackwater Island. I started howling.

"You are making noise," the Sighted Master said.

"The man is going to send me to Blackwater Island!" I cried.

"You are going nowhere," the Sighted Master said. "You are going to sleep under my supervision."

I went back to sleep.

I don't know how long I stayed out of classes, but the next thing I remember is that I was feeling my forehead, from which the bandage had been removed, and the boys had gathered around me to feel it, too. There were impressions on my forehead, and they formed a sort of pattern—two parallel lines of dots, one longer than the other, rather like an elongated Braille "q."

Abdul was feeling it with his fingers, which were as rough as a pumice stone.

I cried out with pain.

" 'Q' for 'quiet'!" he yelled. "Two, four, six, eight, who don't you appreciate? Half-sighted Bhaskar!"

❧

I STARTED getting colds and fevers. "Children often get colds and fevers," Mrs. Ras Mohun said, and she and Mr. Ras Mohun didn't make me stay in bed.

Then I got a bad fever, and they did make me stay in bed.

"Probably the Bombay climate doesn't suit him," Mrs. Ras Mohun said, opening my mosquito net, putting her head in, and feeling my hand.

"It's damp and foggy, and I understand that the Punjab climate is dry and clear," I heard Mr. Ras Mohun say through the mosquito net. "Is that true, Vedi?"

I tried to think about the weather in the Punjab, but I couldn't remember it at all. "It rains here every day," I said.

"But Uncle is asking you about the climate of the Punjab," Mrs. Ras Mohun said.

"I want to go to sleep," I said.

The fever wouldn't go away, and either the next day or the day after that or the day after that—I lost count—Mr. and Mrs. Ras Mohun came to the boys' dormitory with a stranger.

"This is Dr. Bose," Mr. Ras Mohun said. "He is our personal doctor. He has come specially to see you—you remember he came when you had to have stitches in your head?"

"Can you tell what temperature you have?" Dr. Bose asked, opening my pajama coat and putting a cold piece of metal on my chest. He sounded at once very far away and very close, but I decided that he was a Bengali, because he talked like Mr. Ras Mohun—he said "con" for "can," and "hove" for "have." I wanted to laugh.

"Two degrees," I said. I felt very hot.

Dr. Bose laughed. He put an ice-cold thermometer under my tongue. He had a pocket watch. It sounded loud, like a big clock, and I wanted to tell him to put it in the sitting-and-dining room and let me sleep.

I dimly heard him say, "I think he ought to be shifted to a hospital."

I fell asleep.

I woke up in what seemed like the boys' dormitory, except that I could not recognize any of the voices around me. I called for Deoji and for Abdul and for Bhaskar and for Tarak Nath, but no one came to my bedside. I started crying loudly and then checked myself and listened. It seemed that a wall on wheels was being put around my bed.

"It's a prison on Blackwater Island!" I cried.

A lady answered, but either her voice was very quiet or I had begun having difficulty hearing, for I couldn't tell what she was saying.

"What is it?" I called out.

"It's a screen," she said.

I felt cold, unfamiliar hands about my stomach. I

tried to shrink back; the hands, however, were gentle but firm.

"I'm Nurse," the lady said, undoing my pajama string.

I thought that she was going to change my clothes, and I yielded. She took off my pajamas, but instead of giving me new ones she put something cold and metallic under me. Then she pumped me with something that gave me a violent stomach ache. I screamed.

As Daddyji later remembered it, one day he received a letter from Mr. Ras Mohun and, expecting to read Mr. Ras Mohun's usual cheerful, mundane report on me, opened it to find the following message instead:

As from
    Dadar School for the Blind,
      Dadar, Bombay.

22 March, 1939.

Dear Dr. Mehta:

I am sorry to inform you that Vedi was in J. J. Hospital for the past few weeks. The diagnosis was typhoid. I didn't write to you until now because the diagnosis took some time and because I didn't want to alarm you and Mrs. Mehta unnecessarily. He is now perfectly all right and back at the school and running around.

Daddyji was alarmed. He worked in the Public Health Department, and he knew how serious typhoid could be—especially if it was not diagnosed right away. (He had blamed the delay in the diagnosis of meningitis for my blindness.) Moreover, there were several kinds of fever called typhoid, and Mr. Ras Mohun had given no details. But then Daddyji also knew that children in boarding school always came down with one thing or another, and he considered it a good sign that Mr. Ras Mohun had taken the precaution of entering me in J. J. Hospital, which had one of the best medical staffs in Bombay. He also thought it a good sign that Mr. Ras Mohun had given the diagnosis. Many principals in his place would have fudged it. In any case, Daddyji was reassured to learn that I was well again and to read this postscript to Mr. Ras Mohun's letter: "Brother, I regard Vedi as my nephew, and there is nothing Mrs. Ras Mohun and I would not do for him."

Daddyji translated the letter for Mamaji. At the time, she was washing some silk clothes. She remembers that when she heard the word "typhoid" over the rushing water the strength went out of her hands. She says that ever since she saw me off at the station she had felt that I'd entered a different country, like England or America, where Daddyji had gone for his studies—countries of which she had little conception. She had never been to Bombay and had never seen a "blind school." She imagined that it was full of children with bad, watery eyes, about which she also knew next to nothing. The school was run by casteless Christians, she had been told, and she was sure they didn't believe in the influence of the stars or in much of anything else. "Typhoid!" she exclaimed, picking up a dripping veil and trying hard to wring it. Then she added in a small voice, as if comforting herself, "What God wants must be."

Daddyji had already sat down to write Mr. Ras Mohun a letter asking for more details.

❦

Mr. Ras Mohun watched me as I wrote my first letter home, in English, on a Braille slate:

Dadar School for the Blind
Dadar, Bombay.

2 April, 1939.

Dear Daddy and Mummy,
I'm quite well and happy, thank you. How are you?

Your affectionate son,
Vedi

P.S. Typhoid finished.

I took the cardboardlike paper out of the Braille slate and gave it to Mr. Ras Mohun. Then I heard the nib of his pen scratching on the thick paper. I knew he was inking in the message, word for word, between the Braille lines; the boys had told me that that was how a Braille/print letter was written.

I heard him struggling to roll the paper. "If you roll the paper tightly, the roll and the Braille letters will not get crushed in the post," he said. "Can you understand why?"

"Yes, Uncle," I said.

He showed me the rolled-up letter. He had glued

down the free end of the paper and had also put a string through the roll and tied it securely. He took the letter from me and went away to post it.

I remembered how my brother Om's letters used to arrive from his boarding school. They would arrive in small, thin, square envelopes, which rustled like trees in the breeze. They were opened with one quick flick of a letter opener or a finger, and they went on for many pages. I thought of everyone at home struggling with the string and the glued roll of thick Braille paper. I thought of Brother Om's nice, small letter and my unseemly roll both on the mantelpiece, and I felt embarrassed.

VII

ACTIVITIES AND OUTINGS

I T WAS EASTER. WE ALL GATHERED ON THE VERANDA to greet Mrs. Thomas, the school's superinten-dent. We boys stood in one line and the girls stood in another, in front of her and Mr. Ras Mohun, and shouted, "Good morning, Mrs. Thomas!"

"Good morning, boys and girls," she said, in funny-sounding Marathi.

Then she turned to Mr. Ras Mohun, and they started talking together in fast English.

"You hear how respectfully Mr. Ras Mohun talks to her?" Abdul whispered to me. "That's because she's from the rich country of America and has a bigger ruler."

"Thanks to the work of Mrs. Thomas and her good husband, who couldn't be here today," Mr. Ras Mohun was saying to us, "this school is a happy home. Mrs. Thomas would like to hear you sing now."

We boys had never sung together with the girls before, and there was a little confusion about whether they or we should start. But Deoji launched into "When the Saints Go Marching In," and we all joined in.

Then Mrs. Thomas gave a speech. "Boys and girls, I want you all to grow up like Louis Braille," she said, in her funny Marathi. "He was a little boy, like the littlest of you here, who lived in a village far, far away, across the ocean, more than a hundred years ago. He had an accident when he was three years old and went blind. When he was ten, he went to a blind school.

There he learned to read with his fingers something called the line code. At the time, the blind could read the line code, but there was no way for them to write it. Then someone thought up a new code, which could be written. It was a twelve-dot-letter embossed code, and little Louis learned that, but its letters were too big for his fingers and those of his blind friends. So he decided he would think up a better code, and he spent many, many years working on it. He came up with one oblong cell of six embossed dots which could be easily recognized by the littlest fingers. It is because of little Louis that you're able to read and write Braille and go to school. So every night when you go to sleep think of Louis, in Heaven with Jesus, thinking about you."

"Let's give a good cheer for Mrs. Thomas," Mr. Ras Mohun said. "Hip, hip!"

"Hip, hip!" we shouted.

"Hi-i-ip, hip!"

"Hi-i-ip, hip!" we repeated.

"Hurrah!" we all shouted with Mr. Ras Mohun.

Mrs. Thomas thanked us and then came around with a basket and gave everyone a present. Paran got a hand mirror, Abdul got a small wooden cross, Deoji got a small wooden angel, Bhaskar got a rubber frog, and I got a metal car.

Mr. Ras Mohun called on Deoji to thank Mrs. Thomas on behalf of the school.

All of us boys pushed Deoji forward, and he said a few words in English and concluded, "Mrs. Thomas is our saint come marching in. Thank you."

WHENEVER I asked Paran, from the boys' side of the classroom, "What are you doing, Paran?" she would say, "I'm looking into my mirror."

"What do you see in a mirror?"

"My reflection."

"What is that?"

"It's my double."

"But how can it be your double? The mirror is thin and flat."

"You have to be able to see to understand."

I could not work out the puzzle of Paran and the mirror until some time after Abdul and I stumbled onto a heavy stone slab in the cellar. We moved it and discovered that under it was a big, sloping hole. We got down into the hole. I was frightened and wanted to run back, because the tunnel—for that was what it seemed to be—was knee-deep in water, and I could hear things splashing and swimming, scuttling and buzzing. The little noises were picked up and repeated all around me, until it seemed that the whole tunnel was full of ghosts, snakes, and wasps.

"I'm getting out of here!" I shouted.

"I'm getting out of here!" they shouted back.

Abdul and I almost fell over each other getting out of the tunnel.

We put the stone back over the hole and didn't go near it for a few days. But one day I told Deoji about the tunnel.

"That's an old, unused sewer," he said. "I don't know what things were swimming down there. But the sound you heard was an echo."

"What is an echo?"

"It's when your voice bounces back from the walls and the ceiling."

"Why doesn't it do that everywhere?"

"You have to be in a tight corner or the voice will escape."

After that, I would often go down to the slab of stone, move it a chink, and shout, "Hello, there!" As I listened to the echo, I felt that, like Paran, I was looking into a mirror.

ONE AFTERNOON, Mr. Ras Mohun took those of us boys who were totally blind behind the school building, past Abdul's boa-constrictor tree, to a little vacant area by the wall of the Tata Mill. Here he let us feel four waist-high metal wires and what he called the starting and finishing posts, between which the wires had been strung. The wires formed three long lanes, each a few feet wide. Each wire had a hoop about the size of a thick bangle hanging from it.

"This is a racing track," he said. "I have modelled it on a racing track for the blind which I saw at Perkins, in America. We will have races for you here every week."

We were excited. At school, the most we could do was to run up and down the boys' stairs, and even that we were not supposed to do, because the Sighted Master didn't like the noise we made. When we went for our outings, we had to hold on to the partially sighted or half-sighted boys and walk slowly. But here, Mr. Ras Mohun said, we could run, and by ourselves.

Mr. Ras Mohun positioned Abdul, Reuben, and me in separate lanes, at the starting posts, and showed us how to catch hold of the metal hoop by a string that hung from it, and then run with the wire as our guide.

"No, no, Reuben, don't hold on to the string with both hands," Mr. Ras Mohun said. "Just catch hold of the string loosely with your right hand, like this."

"I don't need the string, Uncle," I said. "I can run just holding on to the hoop."

"You need the string for a certain amount of lee-way," he said. "Let's have a trial race, and you'll see what I mean."

I prayed to Jesus, Mary, and Joseph that I would win.

Mr. Ras Mohun called out, "Ready, steady, go!"

I had never run so fast. I imagined myself an arrow flying from one post to the other.

"Oh, my God, they're going to kill themselves!" I heard Mr. Ras Mohun exclaim as I fell sidewise, almost wrapping myself around the finishing post, and hitting my mouth on it.

"Any of you badly hurt?" Mr. Ras Mohun asked, running up to us.

All three of us had bleeding mouths and bleeding foreheads. There had been no way for us to know when we were coming to the end, so we had all fallen down and hurt ourselves on the finishing posts.

Mr. Ras Mohun sent for tincture of iodine and bandages, and after he had attended to our injuries he said, almost to himself, "Bless me, I can't remember how they prevented such mishaps at Perkins." He paused, and then went on, to us, "I know. I'll station the Sighted

Master at the finishing posts with my bell. He can ring it during the races. From the sound of the ringing, you'll know how close you are to the end. As an added precaution, I'll have a nice, strong rope stretched across the lanes, at the height of the wires, just before the end, so that if you fall you won't hit the finishing posts."

After that, every Saturday we had races at the racing track. Mr. Ras Mohun would stand at the starting posts and get us off, and the Sighted Master would stand at the finishing posts, behind the newly stretched rope, and ring the bell. Abdul, Reuben, and I were the three fastest runners, and whenever the school had visitors—missionaries and benefactors, Bombay notables and government officials—we three would be asked to put on a special racing exhibition, running different kinds of races we had learned. We would put on the Biscuit Race: Mr. Ras Mohun would give us each a hard biscuit, and when he said "Ready, steady, go!" we would eat the biscuit quickly, show our mouths to him, and then run. We would put on the Leapfrog Race: we would leap frog-fashion along the racing track, hanging on to the string. We would put on the Dog Race, with two dogs, Bobby and Robby, which Mr. Ras Mohun had just acquired for us to play with: Mr. Ras Mohun would line up Bobby and Robby as best he could outside the lanes, and we would all race against one another. The Dog Race was not as satisfactory as the Biscuit Race or the Leapfrog Race, because Mr. Ras Mohun never quite succeeded in starting Bobby and Robby at the right time and getting them to run exactly as he wanted them to.

As time went on, the boys from a sighted school

nearby occasionally came and joined us at our Saturday races. They would run outside the lanes. I was so eager to compete with them on even terms that now and again I would slyly let go of the string and hurl the hoop forward, so that I could run along the track like them for a time.

❧

ONE WARM DAY, there was a series of explosions at the front gate. At first, I thought someone was setting off firecrackers, but then I realized that what I heard was a motorcar engine idling and repeatedly backfiring. We heard such engine sounds all the time—mixed in with the clip-clop of victoria horses, the clatter of handcarts, and the clink and ponk-ponk of bicycle bells and car klaxons—but they were always the sounds of passing traffic. No vehicle, it seemed, ever stopped in front of the school.

"Mr. Ras Mohun wants us all at the front gate!" Bhaskar cried, running into the boys' dormitory. "There's a lorry! We are really going to Juhu Beach!"

We had heard Mr. Ras Mohun mention the visit to Juhu Beach as a "red-letter day." We had all talked about going to the seaside, without knowing exactly what it was. Abdul had once remarked, "Mahim Sea Beach is not the seaside, and there is no stuffed sand or stuffed ocean for the blind to feel. They have to take us to Juhu Beach to show us what it is."

"Why are we going in a lorry?" I asked now.

"Because there are no trams to Juhu Beach, you son of an owl," Abdul said. "It's really far."

The lorry had no seats, so we all sat on the floor, the boys on one side and the girls on the other. I wanted to run around—perhaps try to sit with Paran—but Mr. Ras Mohun was addressing us from the front of the lorry.

"Boys and girls, this is our first annual holiday at Juhu Beach," he said. "Juhu Beach is on the Arabian Sea, and we have a day's holiday there because of a special gift from Mrs. Thomas and the American Marathi Mission. It will take us quite some time to reach Juhu Beach. I want you to stay in your places, because the ride to Juhu Beach is bumpy."

To help us pass the time, Miss Mary led us in a new song. It really had only one line: "John Brown's Whiskey Bottle Number One Hundred and One." Each time we sang it, we would sing out one number less than the time before. The song sounded naughty and festive to us, and we felt we were really on an annual holiday.

At Juhu Beach, I heard a sound I'd never heard before—a gigantic roar alternating with the sound of a huge amount of water rushing out. The sound was very different from Mahim Sea Beach, which was quiet, like a canal in Lahore. (It was actually an inlet.) I wanted to run toward the sound and touch it—to feel what it was really like—but the Sighted Master herded us boys into the boys' shack. He gave us each a pair of bathing drawers and we got into them.

"Now you can do what you like," the Sighted Master said. "But don't go beyond the rope in the water."

I hesitated for a moment, wondering if there were wired lanes and how, amid the roar and the rush, I would hear the Sighted Master ringing the bell on the other side of the rope, but the partially sighted boys started running toward the roar and the rush, calling back, "Abdul! Reuben! Vedi! There is nothing in the way! You can run, too!"

I ran toward the roar and the rush. The air smelled of salt and coconut. There was hot, grainy, dry ground underfoot. It was so hot that I could scarcely bear to put my feet on it, so I had to run fast, and couldn't stop to examine it. Suddenly, I was in the water, being carried out. It closed over my head. I forgot everything. I felt I'd never been so happy. A jolt opened my mouth. I was rapidly swallowing water that tasted of tears— buckets of them. I was flung back, choking. Again the water closed over my head. The water retreated. I lay on the water, wondering if the sea could take me all the way to the Punjab. Then I came up against the rope, as thick as the one we used for the tug-of-war, and I heard the Sighted Master calling to me, "That's far enough! Come back! You'll drown!"

We spent the day bathing in the water and running around on the new ground. I couldn't get over the way it shifted around, almost like the water. We could go into the water as often as we liked, and when we ran we just had to keep the sound of the ocean to our left or right, depending on which way we were facing. The school compound and the racing track suddenly shrank in my mind, like a woollen sock Mamaji had knitted for me which became so small after Heea's ayah washed it that I could scarcely get my hand in it.

At one point, we had a picnic—Mr. Ras Mohun, the Sighted Master, Mrs. Ras Mohun, Heea, the Matron, and all the boys and girls. We all sat down on bedsheets. For the first time, I was able to sit next to Deoji and eat with him. The food was not mutton and toast but thick, heavy potato-filled bread, with a chewy relish made of pickled mango skin.

❦

IT WAS SUNDAY, and all of us were excited because we had been brought in a fast, sootless electric train to the zoo. We walked in twos and threes along the cages and pens, holding one another or touching the outer railings with our hands. Mr. Ras Mohun explained to us from the front about the animals we were going past while Mrs. Ras Mohun pointed them out to Heea and the partially sighted boys and girls.

"Here is a lion," Mr. Ras Mohun said. "He has a big mane."

"Can I touch him, Uncle?" I asked, running up to him. I had learned the shape of the lion in the birds-and-animals class, but I had no idea how big a lion was. I wondered if the one behind the railing was ten times as big as the stuffed animal in our class, or twenty times, or a hundred times.

"Touch what? The lion?" he asked. "If you touch him, he'll make lunch of your hands, and you'll never be able to read Braille again."

I took a step, and I heard thunder underfoot. I jumped back. "It's going to rain in the ground," I said.

Mr. Ras Mohun laughed. "It's only the lion roaring," he said. "That's the way he talks."

"I didn't know that the lion could make a sound,"
I said. "He sounds as big as our school."

But Mr. Ras Mohun had walked away, and Abdul
said, "You know what he's saying?"

"No. What?"

"He's saying, 'I'm hungry, I want my food.' You
see, the lion is no different from me. Food is all I think
about when I am in my cage at Dadar."

Ahead, Mr. Ras Mohun was walking along and
saying, "Here is a bear. . . . You hear his growl? Notice how different it is from the roar of the lion. . . .
You hear that hooting? Well, that's an owl. . . . Here
are some monkeys."

Mr. Ras Mohun stopped, bought some groundnuts
from a vender, and gave us a few to feed the monkeys.
I put my hand with the nuts inside the railing. Suddenly, I felt a little pinch on my hand, and the nuts
were gone.

"There, Vedi. He's eating the nuts now," Mr. Ras
Mohun said. "You can say now that at least you have
touched a monkey."

Mr. and Mrs. Ras Mohun walked Heea and me
away from the other boys and girls, and took us up a
very tall ladder—it had many more rungs than the
climbing bars at the school—to the top of an elephant.
Here there was a sofa with a cane seat and a cane back,
and we sat on it, facing backward, as in a tonga.

"What's his name?" I asked the mahout, turning
around.

"Dumbo, little Sahib," he said. He clicked his
tongue, as I had heard Lahore tongawallahs do, and the
elephant set off. I expected the elephant to trot, like a

tonga horse, but he rolled and pitched, throwing Mr. and Mrs. Ras Mohun, Heea, and me against one another on the sofa.

I felt I had never been so high up—so close to the sun, which was warm against my cheeks. I felt wonderfully dizzy.

I could hear the voices of Deoji, Abdul, Bhaskar, Tarak Nath, Dham, Miss Mary, and Paran far below. I was riding over the heads of the tallest of them.

"Uncle and Auntie, let's invite Deoji, Abdul, and Paran up," I said.

"The ride on the elephant costs money," Mrs. Ras Mohun said. "And they don't get that much pocket money. Only maharajas can ride elephants."

I recalled that the boys' missionary mummies and daddies sometimes sent them a rupee or two for pocket money on the first day of the month. Even though the boys spent their pocket money only on snacks like mother's kisses at the Muhammadan Hotel, the money was gone before they knew it. Bhaskar would say when he received his money, "This will last me for a month," but within a few days the money would be gone, and he would already be looking forward to the first day of the next month. Then every day he would ask Deoji "How many days to the new month?" and sometimes on the same day "Deoji, when did you say the new month is?"

I wished that Mamaji and Daddyji were there, so they could pay for everyone to ride on Dumbo. I decided that I would count every rung of the ladder on the way down, because then I could tell my friends below how tall the elephant really was.

❧

"WE ARE GOING to the grounds of the Bombay Studios!" Mr. Ras Mohun shouted, standing near the driver of a lorry and addressing all of us, inside it. He had to shout because this lorry was, if anything, noisier than the one that had taken us to Juhu Beach. His thin voice cracked with the effort. "You're going to be actors and actresses in a picture called 'Andhera'! It will be shown in cinemas all over the country!" *Andhera* means "darkness."

I didn't know exactly what a picture was, but I was excited. I expected to meet Cousin Prakash at the cinema place.

The driver changed gears, and for a time I couldn't hear what Mr. Ras Mohun was saying. But then the lorry slowed down, and I heard him say, "Few people have heard of Dadar School. The public doesn't know about schools for the blind. The public doesn't know about the blind. But now Jesus, in his mercy, has given us the cinema to arouse the public's interest in both these matters."

I didn't know what the public was, but I was all the more excited.

The lorry left us in some kind of park. There was no Cousin Prakash; instead, there were a lot of strangers, who surrounded us. They moved us this way and that way, making many of us change places several times.

"You are the smallest," Mr. Ras Mohun said, moving me to the front. "Stand here."

A stranger ran up and pressed down on my shoulders with rough hands. "Down, boy," he said, and I dropped my shoulders. He ran back to where he had been standing, and called out to me, "Boy, look this way. . . . No, no—in the direction of my voice. . . . Now hold up your head. . . . No, that's too high. . . . That's right."

A fly started buzzing around my ear. I tried furtively to flick it with my shoulder.

The stranger with the rough hands shouted, "Stand by. . . . Lights. . . . Action."

A yawn began to fill my mouth, and at the same time my left foot started to fall asleep. The sun was very hot, and lights hot as fire were turned on me. But I didn't move.

"Children of Darkness, come to me. Don't be frightened," I heard a lady say kindly.

I started to step forward.

"Cut!"

"Mr. Ras Mohun, tell him not to move—tell him he's on the set!" the stranger with the rough hands cried.

Mr. Ras Mohun came up to me and put his ruler on my bare arm. It was the first time I had felt it, and, just as Abdul said, it was heavy, round, and hard. "You really mustn't move," Mr. Ras Mohun told me. "You must stand still—at attention."

"But there is a fly!" I cried.

"It won't hurt you. It will go away."

It seemed that we had to do the exercise of standing at attention over and over.

I remember that finally Mr. Ras Mohun called out, "At ease! Boys and girls, you can play now and eat as much *bhel-puri* as you like. The studio's vender will give it to you free."

There was something frightening about eating the secret hot, spicy snacks of the Muhammadan Hotel out in the open, under the eyes of Mr. Ras Mohun. But we ran up to a vender who was crying *"Bhel-puri! Bhel-puri!"* and crowded around him. He handed us *bhel-puri* in plantain leaves. We ate it with our fingers and licked them clean.

Abdul started chasing me. I ran into something, and I felt it to see what it was. It felt like a cart with a mysterious thing on it. I started to climb up on the cart to examine the thing.

The lady with the kind voice came rushing up to me. "You don't want to play with that horrible camera," she said. "Let me show you a better game."

I gave her my hand, and we walked along together. She was very different from Mr. Ras Mohun; she let me walk any way I liked—turning my toes out, running from side to side, falling behind and catching up with her.

"What do you do?" I asked her.

"I am the Lady of Charity in the orphanage in the picture," she said. "You are all my Children of Darkness, and I take care of you."

"Do you know Mrs. Thomas?" I asked, jumping up and down.

"Who is Mrs. Thomas?"

"She's our missionary lady. She came to our school at Easter and brought a present for everyone."

She laughed. "Well, I suppose I'm like her, but in the picture I live in the orphanage."

"What is your new game?" I asked.

"Here it is," she answered. She walked me up a ladder taller than the one on the elephant. Then she sat me down at the top and pushed me. I laughed and shrieked with delight, for I was on a slide and it seemed endless. Every time I thought I had come to the bottom of the slide, it turned out to be only a landing and there was another slope. The school slide had one slope, but this slide had many slopes.

"Again!" I cried when I reached the bottom. I was so light-headed I could scarcely stand up.

"That's enough for today," she said. "You can go on the slide again tomorrow."

Every day for the next month or two, the lorry came for us and took us to the cinema place. Every day, we had to stand still under the hot sun near the fire of lights. Every day, there was a lot of *bhel-puri* to eat and many rides down the slide. But, for some reason, except for these few memories of routine—and, of course, the remarkable first day—I remember little about "Darkness." (According to the National Film Archive of India, the film eventually made was quite different: "The story tells the heart rending saga of Jyoti—a girl —who is caught in a dilemma between her lover who blames her for being ungrateful and cause for his blindness and a father, who blames her for deserting her blind father and blind sister. She serves them both in disguise as a nurse and eventually her lover on regaining his sight realises the folly committed by him in judging Jyoti.")

VIII

HOLIDAYS

M RS. RAS MOHUN PUT SOMETHING IN MY BOWL. "Now eat your porridge," she said.

"I want some banana," I said.

"You know perfectly well there are no bananas these days," she said. "There is a war on."

"Mr. Anand is coming today," Mr. Ras Mohun said. "He's going to take you to Lahore for your Christmas holidays."

For a moment, I couldn't remember who Mr. Anand was. As soon as I remembered that he was Cousin Prakash, I didn't want to meet him. He was a sahib, like Mr. Ras Mohun. I was a blind boy from the boys' dormitory. I thought that I had forgotten Punjabi and that he would laugh at my Marathi. I thought that he would make fun of the boys' dormitory.

"What are Deoji, Abdul, Bhaskar, and Paran going to do for their Christmas holidays?" I asked. "I want to stay with them. I don't want to meet Cousin Prakash."

"Most of them will stay with us here at the school—they don't have loving parents, a brother, and sisters to go to—but there will be no classes during the holidays," Mr. Ras Mohun said.

"I'm not going home," I said, playing with my porridge and taking a small spoonful to please Mrs. Ras Mohun. "I don't know Punjabi."

"You'll pick it up quickly," Mr. Ras Mohun said.

"We should have got him some fruit for his porridge today," Mrs. Ras Mohun said to Mr. Ras Mohun. "It's his last day of school."

"School is nice. I want to stay in the boys' dormitory," I said.

"Now go and pack," Mr. Ras Mohun said. "Deoji will help you."

❦

AT LAHORE STATION, it seemed that about ten people had picked me up at once and were kissing me and handing me to one another. I stiffened. I didn't like to be picked up or touched, and I couldn't tell exactly who was who. The voices around me sounded familiar, but I heard them distantly. Everywhere there was a deafening racket of engines shunting, of handcarts rattling past, of people shouting.

"Vedi sobbed most of the way," I heard Cousin Prakash say, in Punjabi, over the station din. "He says he has forgotten Punjabi and doesn't know how he's going to speak to you."

Everyone laughed.

"You think you've grown so big that you can't talk to your own mummy?" Mamaji said, pressing me against her neck. She said "mummy," in English, as if a boy coming from a boarding school would naturally call her Mummy instead of Mamaji.

In the quiet of the car, I touched the dashboard and touched the steering wheel. I listened to the soothing murmur of the engine and suddenly asked, in Punjabi, "Where is my ayah, Ajmero?"

"She's gone," Mamaji said, hugging me in her lap.

"Gone where?"

"To her village."

I kept on asking about Ajmero.

After I went blind, when I needed something I would often run to Ajmero instead of to Mamaji; I couldn't think of Mamaji without fearing pain, because Mamaji took me to faith healers who prescribed stinging solutions to restore my sight and beat me with birch twigs to exorcise the evil eye. When Ajmero washed clothes in a basin in the inside courtyard, she would let me sit with her on the ground. She would hand me a glass containing a little bit of the soapy water from her basin. As she kneaded the clothes, I would blow soap bubbles through a glass bead that she had pinched for me from a beaded curtain, and pretend I was helping her wash clothes. I would listen to the tinkle of the dozens of glass bangles she always wore on her arms, and try to gurgle into the glass to accompany the tinkling. I never knew how big the bubble at the end of my bead was, and I would go on blowing to make it bigger and bigger. When it burst, she would go into peals of laughter and say, "That was really a big bubble! Blow another one." I liked the sounds we made together washing clothes. When Ajmero was making biscuits in the kitchen, she would let me cut out the dough with biscuit cutters. I liked running my fingers along the dough cutouts and feeling the different shapes—a hillock, a star, a half-moon. I liked to wait around for the baking smells to rise and fill the kitchen. At night, Ajmero would sit by my bed and sing me to sleep. She knew a few village lullabies, and she sang them in a lilting voice. Sometimes when I was going off to sleep, I would feel that she was singing inside my head. I couldn't remember thinking about Ajmero at all at school, but now, in the car, I remembered all at once her bangles, her laughter, the soap bubbles, the hillocks, the stars, the half-moons, the lullabies.

"When is Ajmero coming back?" I asked.

"She's not coming back," Mamaji said.

"Why not?"

From the back seat, my big sisters, Pom, Nimi, and Umi, tried to divert me, but I wouldn't be diverted.

"She went to her village to visit her people," Daddyji finally said, from the driver's seat. "She fell asleep under a shisham tree. There was a sudden dust storm. The tree fell on her, and the poor girl died immediately. The tree must have been old. Its roots must have been eaten by worms. The tree must have struck her on the head. Perhaps the dust storm was more violent—"

"She was a foolish girl," Sister Umi broke in. "Lying under an old tree in the middle of a dust storm! I always thought she was a little silly."

"She wasn't silly!" I cried.

"Poor girl, she was hardly sixteen," Mamaji said. "So young and simple. How she used to like to go out dressed in my saris! The ayahs of other families would scold her for taking liberties, and she would say, 'I take out my mistress's children, don't I? If their ayah is not well dressed, what will people think?'"

"Here we are—home, sweet home," Daddyji said, stopping the car.

I went from room to room, quietly calling Ajmero.

A man picked me up in the inside courtyard. I struggled to get down.

"You don't remember who I am?" he asked.

"I don't," I said. "I don't like you. Let me down."

"I am your old servant." He took my hand and put it on his right ear. There, hanging from his earlobe, was a small ring.

As soon as I touched it, I remembered. "You are Sher Singh!" I cried.

"It's so. It's your same Sher Singh."

"The tiger-lion with an earring!" I exclaimed, laughing. "Are you going to eat up Baby Usha?" He, like Ajmero, had come to work at our house when my little sister, Usha, was born. He had told me that Sher Singh meant "tiger-lion." After that, I used to call him "the tiger-lion with an earring" and tease him about eating up Baby Usha.

"How could Huzoor forget?" he said. "Ajmero is gone, like your eyes, Vedi Sahib, but I'm still here to play with you."

He brought out of the kitchen a strip of rubber from an old bicycle tube and a forked stick, and showed me how to loop the rubber around the stick and fashion a slingshot. He showed me how to aim a stone at crows and kites from the little lawn in the front, always being careful to face away from the house and to make sure no one was about.

"Drowned one, he'll break all our windows!" Mamaji shouted to Sher Singh from the veranda. "Drowned one" is a common Punjabi term of abuse.

Sher Singh quickly secreted the slingshot, but whenever Mamaji went out he would give it to me. I would go out on the lawn, collect a pile of stones, listen for the cawing of crows or the shrieking of kites, and take aim. I don't remember ever hitting a bird, but just the sound of the rubber snapping, releasing the stone into the air, and then of the stone ricocheting off a wall delighted me. I came to think that shooting with my toy weapon was a much more grownup game than washing clothes had been.

I WAS ABLE TO PREVAIL upon Sister Pom to clear a shelf in a cupboard for me and to let me arrange my knickers, shirts, and socks exactly as I had arranged them in my suitcase at school. But no matter how often I told Mamaji that I wanted to wash my knees and elbows myself, she would catch hold of me and start scrubbing them. "Let Mummy do it for you," she would say. No matter how often I told Sher Singh that I wanted to make my own bed, he would make it for me. "What are servants for?" he would say. "If I don't make Vedi Sahib's bed, what will I do with my time?" No matter how often I told the sweeper that I wanted to polish my own shoes, she would polish them. "Sahib, we are poor people," she would say. "Such jobs are for us. You are big people. Such jobs are not even for your notice." So I had to get used to letting things be done for me. But I could not get used to doing without the school bell. Without it, I never knew what time it was.

"Sher Singh, what time is it?" I would shout.

"I don't know, Vedi Sahib. It must be twelve or one."

"Which is it—twelve or one?"

"Sahib, I am a poor man. I don't have a watch. Why don't you ask the sahibs and memsahibs?"

I would run from room to room trying to get someone to tell me the time, but more often than not Mamaji's watch had stopped, Sister Pom's watch was too slow, Sister Nimi had forgotten to wear her watch, and Daddyji was nowhere to be found. (Brother Om was too small to own a watch.)

Sister Umi had the correct time but wouldn't tell me what it was. "Why do you always want to know what time it is?" she would say. "You're not at school. You have nothing to do all day. What difference does it make?"

I couldn't explain what difference it made, but I would pull at her wrist and order her to tell me the time.

"Go order someone else around," she would say.

Eventually, I worked out my own system for telling time. When I heard the sweeper washing the drain in the *gulli* in front of our house in the morning, I knew that it was eight o'clock and time to get up. When I heard the vender Jhanda calling "Oranges, pomegranates, guavas!" at our gate, I knew that it was nine o'clock and time for breakfast. When I heard the radio announcer come on after the request program of film songs—Brother Om's favorite—I knew that it was one o'clock and time for lunch. When I heard the frenetic ringing of a bicycle bell with the call "Carry-home ice cream, carry-home ice cream!" coming down the *gulli,* I knew that it was four o'clock and time for tiffin. And when I heard the "Beep, beep, beep, beep, beep bee-eep" of the BBC—Daddyji always listened to the news in English—I knew that it was nine o'clock and half an hour to dinner.

It was one thing to know the time and quite another to get everyone to do things on time. On top of our house were some laborers who were reinforcing the roof with steel and cement, and I got them to shape the end of a steel rod into a hook. I put a string through the hook and suspended the rod from a nail in the inside courtyard. I got another rod for a striker. At mealtimes, I would hit the striker against the hanging rod and shout "Sher Singh, where is my breakfast?" and "Sher Singh, bring my lunch!" and "Sher Singh, you know I like my tiffin on the table at four o'clock sharp!" If Sher Singh didn't answer at once, I would go on ringing my bell until everyone in the house was shouting at him to obey my orders. If Sher Singh was still tardy, I would clench my teeth, close my lips tightly, and go on ringing the bell furiously. But, I remember, I would not allow my eyes to tear.

"Why don't you ever cry?" Sister Umi finally asked me.

"Daddyji will beat me."

"What rubbish! Has he ever beaten anybody?"

"He has a ruler."

"Who has a ruler?"

"Uncle."

"Which uncle?"

"Uncle Ras Mohun."

"What are you talking about?"

I started crying, tears suddenly streaming down my cheeks and neck.

ONE EVENING at the table, I raised my little finger. Nobody paid any attention. I raised my fourth finger, too. Still nobody paid any attention. I cleared my throat several times.

"What do you think you are doing?" Sister Umi asked. "Why are you holding your hand up in that absurd way?"

"Water and vegetables," I whispered. "Little finger for water, both fingers for water and food."

"Speak up," she said. "Why are you whispering? Why don't you say, 'I want water and vegetables'?"

"That's what jungly boys do."

"Which jungly boys?" Sister Umi asked. "Who says that?"

"Auntie at school says it."

"Who? Mrs. Ras Mohun?" Sister Umi asked. "She must talk a lot of nonsense. She must be an odd duck!"

I pictured Mrs. Ras Mohun as a duck in the birds-and-animals class, and I laughed out loud.

"Why are you laughing with your hand across your mouth?" Sister Umi asked. "Someone would think that you were sneezing or yawning."

"Only jungly boys laugh without covering their mouths," I said, sobering a little.

"No doubt that's another of Mrs. Ras Mohun's brilliant ideas," she said.

"Here, Vedi, hold my hands." Sister Nimi said, laughing. "Now, see—I am laughing, and my hands are nowhere near my mouth."

Daddyji happened to arrive from his club just then, and when he learned what we had been talking about he said, "If you want to ask for things by raising your hand, you can—Mrs. Ras Mohun probably taught you to raise your hand for things because she didn't want you to be rude and interrupt—but you are in your own home now, and you should feel free to interrupt at any time and call for whatever you want. As for that laughing business, I've been right around the world, and I've never seen anybody laugh with a hand across the mouth. And the next time I write to Mrs. Ras Mohun I'll tell her so."

After that, I hardly ever raised my hand for water and food, and I tried to laugh without covering my mouth, but sometimes when I was laughing my hand would go up to my mouth automatically.

It seemed that at the table everyone was always referring to things that had happened while I was away. I remember that once my big sisters were all laughing.

"Nimi really behaved like a simpleton," Sister Pom said. "Imagine saying, 'If the tigers are coming, let's all climb up the trees.' "

"Which tigers? Where?" I asked. "Can't they climb trees? Where were you?"

But they wouldn't stop to explain; they had already gone on to something else. When I persisted, Sister Umi said, "I'll tell you later."

I beat my spoon on my plate and insisted on being told right then.

"We were just on a walk and it got dark," Sister Pom said. "We thought we were lost, and Umi thought tigers would come and eat us all up."

"What else do you want to know?" Sister Umi asked.

I thought I wanted to know much more, but I couldn't remember what. I tried to get them to remind me of exactly what they had been talking about, but Sister Umi said, "How do you expect us to remember what you want to know?"

They went on to some other subject.

ONE DAY, DADDYJI bought six picture albums, one for each of us brothers and sisters. They were small oblong affairs with cushioned bindings and came with packets of little corners to hold the pictures in the album.

There was one particular picture that I wanted very much for my album. But there was only one copy, and Sister Umi had appropriated it and wouldn't give it to me.

"Why do you want the picture?" she said. "You can't see it. Why do you even need the album?"

"I can, too, see the picture," I said defiantly. I had imagined that I could see it ever since I heard the story about how it came to be taken.

When I was at school, my big sisters had gone to Karachi with Bhabiji, our paternal grandmother, and stayed with Cousin Prakash, who had got into the Customs Department and was posted for a time as an Assistant Collector of Customs there. His younger sister Shanti was in the marriage market, and it seemed that every day she would trot off to the studios to have a formal portrait taken for prospective suitors. My big sisters became jealous of all the attention she was getting. They got Bhabiji to ask Cousin Prakash to have one formal photograph taken of Bhabiji with the three of them. "Sure, Bhabiji," Cousin Prakash said. "Let's have a photograph of you with all your granddaughters who are here—Shanti, Pom, Nimi, and Umi." But Sister Umi said, "Shanti is the daughter of Bhabiji's daughter. Bhabiji wants one formal portrait with only the daughters of her eldest son." And so, as Sister Umi later boasted, a formal portrait was taken in the studio, with Bhabiji dressed in her best white cottons and my big sisters dressed in new satin suits sewn for the occasion. Cousin Shanti sulked because she thought she had been bested, but my big sisters felt elated.

"I want that picture for my album," I repeated.

"Umi, give it to him," Sister Nimi said. "What difference does it make?"

"It's my picture," Sister Umi said. "I was the one who got Bhabiji to have it taken."

I appealed to Daddyji. He said that a second print should be made for me. But the negative had been misplaced, and I lost all interest in getting a new negative made after Sister Umi told me, "Your print will be inferior to my original copy."

Night after night, when I went to bed, I prayed to Jesus, Mary, and Joseph to help me wrest the picture from Sister Umi, but I never got it.

❦

"HERE IS A LETTER for you," Sister Pom said. "It's from your friend Deoji."

I was embarrassed. I hardly ever mentioned him or anyone else from the boys' dormitory. They belonged in a school for the blind, not in the house of a sighted, well-to-do family. "Give it to me," I said. I put out my hand, thinking that I could quietly read it by myself.

"But it's not in Braille," she said. "It's written in ink, and it's in English."

Before I could think of an excuse to take the letter away from Sister Pom, she read out, "My dear Vedi, Mr. Ras Mohun is to saying that an idle mind is to being the Devil's workshop, and that there are to being no people more likely to getting up to Devil-things than the blind sort. So he is to organizing all kinds of things to keeping us busy. We are to washing the floors, walls, windows, doors, and such. We are also to cleaning up every bed frame with Lifebuoy soap and water. Your special bed is to getting a good airing. The pupil-teachers, Miss Mary and Mr. Joseph, are to studying the new Braille primer for the new year. Mr. Ras Mohun is to getting for us two gentlemen, Mr. Draughtswallah and Mr. Cardswallah. Mr. Draughtswallah and Mr. Cardswallah are to coming every day and to teaching us two indoor games, draughts and cards. We are to spending much time to playing them. I have to deciding to teaching you draughts and cards so that you are not to falling behind. Mr. Ras Mohun is also to buying for us a radio. The Matron is to in charging of it, and she is to turning it on at news times in the veranda in the evenings. So we are to getting very busy and happy here. The boys' dormitory is to requesting to you to bringing new toys. The Sighted Master is to asking your Daddy-Doctor for to sleep medicine. Everyone is to missing you and to counting the days for your to coming back to school. The boys' dormitory is to sending you good health and wishes. Mr. Draughtswallah, who is to knowing English and to writing this letter for me, is to sending you his compliments. Your affectionate Loving Big Brother, Deoji."

Sister Pom handed me the letter. "He sounds nice. He must be a nice boy," she said.

I ran out of the room and pushed the letter as far back as I could under the shelf paper and clothes in my cupboard.

IX

BRAILLE PICTURES

Family group, Simla, 1934
Top row: Om, Daddyji, Umi
Bottom row: Pom, Mamaji with Vedi, Nimi

A NOTHER WINTER, ANOTHER RIDE TO THE LAHORE
station, another family gathering on the platform. Again I remember the train hooting.
Again I remember being passed from Daddyji's
arms to Mamaji's and back and feeling frightened. I cried. I protested. I shouted over the din
of the station. I screamed, "I don't want to go back to
school!" Daddyji explained to me, as he had before, that
he was being transferred to another public-health post,
that my big sisters and my big brother, therefore, were
also going to boarding school, that he had kept me back
from school for a whole year to build up my health, that
I would be seven years old soon, and that every boy of
seven went to school. Mamaji tried to divert me by
rattling the bottle of sleeping medicine that Daddyji
had given me for the Sighted Master and by enumerat-
ing the clay and wooden presents she had bought for
me to give to my school friends.

A beggar came up. The coolie minding my lug-
gage tried to shoo him away. Mamaji whispered fast to
Daddyji, as if she didn't want me to hear, "Give him
something. He's blind."

I remember thinking that I could end up like him,
and feeling even more frightened.

Suddenly, I was in the compartment and the train
was pulling away, the wheels clattering insistently as
the train gathered speed, the rhythmic, steady chug and
lurch sounding more and more forlorn as the familiar
sounds of the station faded and vanished. I was leaving

the others behind, but I felt that I had been left behind, in the train.

In the compartment with me this time was not Cousin Prakash but his garrulous younger brother Cousin Dev, who was on leave from the university where he was studying. He sang film songs, drummed on the compartment wall in accompaniment, talked to himself, and tickled me on the back of my neck. At station after station, I begged him to buy me some sugar-coated anise seeds, but he wouldn't, saying, "Vedi, you might as well ask me to throw away good money."

When we reached the school, Cousin Dev insisted that he wanted to give everyone his present himself, and he made a ceremony of presenting the sleeping medicine to the Sighted Master and choosing the clay pitcher for Deoji, the clay god for Abdul, the wooden apple for Bhaskar, the wooden horse for Tarak Nath. He spent a night at the school, staying in Mr. and Mrs. Ras Mohun's sleeping quarters.

"I've never encountered so many mosquitoes and mosquito bites in one place," he said at the breakfast table. He sat with Mr. and Mrs. Ras Mohun at their table, while I took my old place at my little separate table. "All night, I was either fighting off mosquitoes or dreaming I was fighting off mosquitoes. At last count, I had at least sixteen mosquito bites." Apparently, Mr. and Mrs. Ras Mohun did not have an extra mosquito net, for Cousin Dev's cot.

"It's the Bombay climate," Mr. Ras Mohun said.

"It's the Dadar area," Mrs. Ras Mohun said.

"But you can tell Dr. Mehta that we are spraying

the school regularly with insecticide, and the mosquito conditions are getting better," Mr. Ras Mohun said.

As Cousin Dev was leaving for the station to take the train back home, he said to me, "Well, Vedi, they say boarding schools make men out of boys. No one could stay a boy long here, with all these mosquitoes."

❧

ONE MORNING WHEN I was sitting at my separate table in the Ras Mohuns' sitting-and-dining room, I started eating with my fingers.

"Not like that," Mrs. Ras Mohun said. "Eat with your spoon. Going home has made you forget everything."

"I don't like spoons," I said.

"You need to be retrained," she said.

"Overfond parents always tend to spoil blind children," Mr. Ras Mohun said.

That morning, I refused to bathe under the tap of cold water and demanded a bucket of hot water from the Sighted Master.

Mr. Ras Mohun scolded me when he heard about it, saying, "Your parents are overfond. You have to be retrained."

I soon learned that there was no point in refusing to eat with a spoon or to bathe in cold water—there was no one to run to with my complaints and appeals. Besides, I wanted to be a good child, like Heea. In my absence, she had grown big, and she was now talking a lot. Mr. Ras Mohun was writing a book of poems about her, and she had taken to reciting one of them:

> There was a little girl
> Who had a pretty curl
> Falling on her forehead.
> Her hair was nicely plaited
> With a ribbon long and red
> That sweet jasmines bedecked.

She had started school and had acquired, besides the ribbon in her hair, a set of colored pencils and a picture book. "I go to a real school," she said one day when we were waiting for Mr. and Mrs. Ras Mohun to come in for tiffin. "See, I've got a real book with a tape to mark the page. You want me to tell you this picture?"

"No, I don't," I said.

"You have Braille pictures?"

"Of course we do," I said, trying to imagine what a Braille picture could be like.

"Can I see one?"

"You're too small."

"Heea is big now—Heea goes to school," she said. "You want me to draw you a color picture?"

"No."

"You have Braille color pictures?"

"Of course."

"Can I see?"

"Later."

"When? Today?"

"When you grow up."

"I am big. I go to a real school."

"What's the name of your school?"

"Scottish Orphanage."

"Who goes there?"

"Good families. You want to come to my school? You want to play with my colored pencils?"

I decided that, next to Paran, Heea was the nicest girl about, but also that I would just as soon play with Abdul and Deoji in the boys' dormitory.

IN THE BRAILLE CLASS, we had two new Braille books. Besides "Bible Stories for Boys and Girls," we now had the "Reading Primer for Small Children," with a rough cloth cover, and "Fairy Tales for Small Children," with a thin cardboard cover. The "Fairy Tales" had a narrow felt tape to mark the page, just like Heea's book.

One day, Deoji brought a new boy to the Braille class. "This is Raj," Deoji said. "Mr. Ras Mohun has sent him. He is here to learn Braille."

We all gathered around Raj to touch him. He was a few inches taller than I was, and his clothes were as soft as mine.

"Be careful," Deoji said. "He's a special student, from a cultured home, like Vedi."

"My father is an eye specialist," Raj said. He had a small, hesitant voice, like someone who had never gone to school before.

"Feel his eyes," Abdul suddenly said. "They're watering. He's a crybaby."

"They water all the time," Raj said. "I can't help it."

We laughed. We were dry-eyed except when we were crying, and the idea of someone who cried all the time was funny.

"I know why you cry so much," Abdul said. "It's because you must rub your eyes."

"I can't help rubbing them," Raj said. "They hurt."

All of us were always banging into something and hurting someplace or other, and Raj's idea that if you rubbed what hurt, the hurt would go away sounded really funny.

"You're a very strange boy," Abdul said.

Instead of protesting, Raj said, "I'm going to be a day scholar."

"What's that?" we cried.

"You know, it's someone who comes for classes and then goes home."

Except for me, none of us boys had a home, and I had come to school by taking a train for a night and a day and more. The idea that Raj could come to classes from his home the way we came to classes from the boys' dormitory seemed extremely odd.

"I think they are going to have an empty bed in the boys' dormitory," Bhaskar said. "Sickly Ramesh is not long for the boys' dormitory. You could have his bed."

Raj didn't seem to understand what Bhaskar was saying. When he finally did, he said, "I don't want to live in your boys' dormitory. In fact, I don't want to go to your school. I am just here for six months, until I learn the fundamentals of Braille. Then I'll go back to my old sighted school. I've already studied there for four years. You see, I only just lost my sight."

So far, no one we knew of had left the school, and we were puzzled.

"He'll think better of it," Abdul said. "He'll be here learning his funmentals, or whatever it is, until he's as old as Deoji and Reuben."

Everyone laughed.

In subsequent days, Raj, just as he had said, came for classes and left after them. Every morning, he arrived in a victoria, and every afternoon he left in a victoria—like a big sheikh. We were all impressed, because even Mr. Ras Mohun didn't take victorias. But Raj was so clumsy that he couldn't get from the victoria to the classroom, or from the classroom to the boys' common bathroom, without one of us escorting him.

Mr. Ras Mohun said to me, "Finally, you have a friend from a cultured home," and he always made Raj sit next to me. I took charge of Raj and showed him around the school. I showed him Mr. Ras Mohun's office and Mrs. Ras Mohun's flower-and-vegetable bed. I told him about the Sighted Master's snoring and the school ghosts at night. I took him up to the boys' dormitory and introduced him as best I could to Jaisingh. I told him about walks to Mahim Sea Beach, about the annual trip to Juhu Beach, about running at the racing track. I even told him something I hadn't thought of until the moment I said it—that when I grew up I was going to marry Paran. But Raj didn't get excited about any of it.

And the most surprising thing of all was that one day, after a few months, he stopped coming, without even saying goodbye. Every day, we waited for the sound of his victoria at the gate, but it never came.

❧

THE BIRDS-AND-ANIMALS class was now held only on alternate days, and on the other days we had a new class with Miss Mary, geography and arithmetic. In one of the first geography-and-arithmetic classes, Miss Mary introduced us to a new toy—a boxlike affair with a needle on it that we could push around and fix at any point. It was called a teaching compass, and we all took turns playing with it.

"When the needle points to me, it's pointing north," Miss Mary told us. "When it points to you, it's pointing south."

With the help of the compass, she taught us not only north and south but also east and west, northeast, northwest, southeast, and southwest.

Then, one day, she gave each of us what felt like the oblong brass tray that Sher Singh generally used when he collected glasses at home. The top of the tray-like thing, however, was punched out with rows upon rows of little holes, like a pegboard.

"Those are arithmetic slates," Miss Mary told us.

"But it doesn't have any beads," Paran said.

"You are all too advanced for an abacus now," Miss Mary said. "Instead of beads, an arithmetic slate has type."

Miss Mary went around the room and gave us each a handful of type. Each type was a little square peg with a raised edge on one end and two prongs on the

other. Miss Mary showed us that when a type was inserted at different angles in a hole in the arithmetic
slate, either with the raised edge up or with the prongs
up, it felt different under our fingers. In subsequent
lessons, we learned that the different directions a raised
edge faced signified different numbers: 1 was made by
facing the raised edge northeast; 2 by facing it due east;
3 by facing it southeast; 4 by facing it due south; 5 by
facing it southwest; 6 by facing it due west; 7 by facing
it northwest; 8 by facing it due north. To make 9, we
inserted the type prongs up, with the prongs facing
northeast, in the manner of 1. Similarly, 0 was made by
facing the prongs due east, in the manner of 2. When 1
and 0 were placed next to each other in a row, they
made 10, and so on. The other angles with the prongs
up were used as signs for addition, subtraction, multiplication, and division. When we wanted to add or sub-
tract numbers, we were to place numbers on rows, one
under another, and skip a row of holes before putting
in the answer. We were to follow a similar procedure
for multiplication and division.

At first, we had trouble separating directions from
numbers. I remember that once Miss Mary asked us to
add 21 and 24, and I quickly cried out, "The answer is
south-southwest!"

"Forty-south," Paran corrected me.

"I wish I had never mentioned directions to you
along with numbers," Miss Mary said. "Southwest was
only an analogy."

"What is an analogy, Miss Mary?" Abdul asked.

"Never you mind, Abdul. What is the answer?"

"I don't know," Abdul said. "It's three."

"What's wrong with your coconut, Abdul?" Miss Mary scolded. "Bhaskar, what is the answer?"

Miss Mary went around the classroom, asking everyone, but no one gave the correct answer.

"The correct answer is forty-five," Miss Mary said.

"I think it would be much easier if we did our sums in Braille," Abdul said.

"In Braille, you can't erase," she said. "On an arithmetic slate, you can change numbers almost with the flick of a finger. The whole process is twenty times as fast and easy."

THE BOYS' DORMITORY was a changed place, thanks to some new indoor games. Almost the first day I was back at school, Deoji said, "Let me teach you how to play cards."

"Cards? What kind of cards?"

"Playing cards."

I was surprised. I had thought that only grownups could play cards, and then only grownups who could see. At home, Mamaji would play rummy with a circle of friends. I would stand at her elbow and ask, "What card did you put down? You promised to call out its name."

"Oh, I forgot. Ten of spades."

The next time, she would again forget to call out the card. Her friends didn't even try. If I asked them what cards they had put down, they would say, "Go outside and play with your mouth organ."

Whenever I asked Mamaji questions about how

the game was played, she would say, "It's not for you. It's a grownup game.

"But is the ace higher than the king?" I would ask.

"Sometimes it's higher than the king, and sometimes it's lower than the deuce."

"How can it be both?"

"It just is—it depends."

"It depends on what?"

"It depends on what you want it to be—on what else you have in your hand."

No matter how often I asked her, it seemed that she couldn't explain the game to me, and after a while I lost interest in it. I made up my own game in my head, in which diamonds were Mamaji's jewelry, hearts were tokens of naughty love, a club was where Daddyji went, and a spade was what we used to turn the soil in Mrs. Ras Mohun's flower-and-vegetable bed.

Then Mamaji got the idea that if I touched the cards it would bring her good luck, and now and again she would call me and give me the deck to shuffle. At first, I was clumsy and would either spill the cards or shuffle them in batches. But I quickly learned to hold the two halves of the deck edge to edge and flip them rapidly. I came to love the sound. It was like the sound of dozens of sparrows flying away from a tree.

Now Deoji handed me a playing card. On the top left corner was "gd" in Braille, and the same letters were written on the bottom right corner.

"That is the seven of diamonds," Deoji said. He explained that "g" stood for seven (in Braille, letters also have to stand for numbers) and "d" for diamond, that "a" was ace and "k" was king and "q" was queen and "j" was jack, and that "h" was hearts and "c" was clubs and "s" was spades.

In the following days, he taught me rummy, and we started playing it. It seemed so simple. Every time we put down a card, we had to call out its name; for the rest, the game was a matter of collecting three of this and a sequence of that.

After one of our early games, I shuffled the deck.

"I didn't know you could shuffle," Deoji said.

I told him about Mamaji.

"But Braille cards should not be shuffled as ordinary cards are, because then you might rub out the Braille dots," Deoji said. "Braille cards are best shuffled by pulling out a batch at a time and putting it on top."

Playing cards became a common pastime for me in the dormitory, stopped being magical, stopped conjuring up Mamaji's diamonds and Daddji's clubs.

In my absence, the boys, in addition to learning to play cards, had learned a new indoor game called draughts. I picked up the game quickly. It had a big cardboard playing board with recessed circles and was played with many small discs, called men, and a few double-height discs, called kings. A man could "eat" an enemy's man by jumping over him if that man's back was left unprotected, and a man was crowned a king when he reached the back row of the enemy's side. Half the men and half the kings were marked with smooth metal buttons on top and were called white. The other half had no buttons on top and were called black. In the boys' dormitory, there was only one draughts set— Mr. Ras Mohun had obtained it from the Royal National Institute for the Blind, in England—and on week-ends we used to sit around on our beds waiting to take our turn, rushing along the boys who were playing with shouts of "Hurry up!" and "Why are you taking so long with your move?"

As I waited for my turn, I would remember my big sisters and my big brother and my cousins gathered around a ludo or Monopoly board, talking in rapid English, their games as mysterious as their language. They would give me a few counters and pieces to play with. I would move them on the floor and show an imaginary blind partner where I had put everything, but it had never occurred to me that there could be an indoor game like ludo or Monopoly which I could play with real people. And now here was draughts, and I was being called to play with Abdul. We tossed a coin and I got the white, and our hands covered the board, feeling all the men in their recessed circles—like so many soldiers in foxholes, as Deoji said. At one point, one of my men jumped and ate one of Abdul's men, and as I waited for Abdul to make his next move I thought of my men as Englishmen with smooth metal helmets and Abdul's men as bareheaded Indians. I imagined I was a king myself, waiting to be crowned in Abdul's back row.

THERE WAS ALSO a new outdoor game that had been introduced in my absence—one for which Mr. Ras Mohun had bought a special ball. The ball was a hollow thick-rubber thing about four inches across with big round holes cut into it here and there. In through the holes Mr. Ras Mohun had forced a few bottle tops, which clinked when the ball rolled along the ground.

When I first felt the ball, I was disappointed. "I want a ball like Brother Om's," I said to Deoji, and I told him about Brother Om's ball. It was three or four times the size of Mr. Ras Mohun's ball. It had a bladder with a tube and had to be filled with a bicycle pump. It had a little hollow for tucking in the tube, a tongue for closing up the hollow, and a lace for tying down the tongue. All around the ball were seams that made a nice design on it. It had such a lively bounce that you could hear it bouncing along all the way down the *gulli* and follow it by the sound. Sometimes it kept bouncing until I couldn't hear it anymore. Mr. Ras Mohun's ball had hardly any bounce. It rolled along the ground like a kicked stone.

"For a ball like your brother's, you would need a long *gulli* or a huge compound to play in," Deoji told me. "Mr. Ras Mohun's ball is right for us, because what the blind sort here need is a ball that rolls slowly in our little front courtyard."

After that, I began to enjoy playing the ball game that Mr. Ras Mohun had thought up for us. He would stand on the steps of the veranda and throw the ball toward the gate. We would take turns, in twos and threes, dashing to find the ball by the clinks of the bottle tops. We would run into one another, fall over one another, and fight to be the first to grab the ball and run with it to Mr. Ras Mohun, while he cheered us on in his little falsetto: "Come on, boys! . . . Go after it! . . . That's it! . . . This way! . . . Here is my hand!"

If I got the ball before Abdul, he would cry out

"You dog!" In fact, sometimes, when we were sure Mr. Ras Mohun was not within earshot, one of us would stand on the veranda steps, hold back Bobby and Robby, throw the ball, let go of the dogs, and shout like Mr. Ras Mohun (we had no trouble imitating his voice, since many of us had high, thin voices), "Come on, dogs! Go after it!" Then we would stand on the steps with our hands outstretched for the ball as the dogs scurried and leaped, growled and barked.

X

A DISTANT PROSPECT

D ADDYJI HAD BEEN CORRESPONDING WITH MR. RAS
Mohun, asking him for his help in getting me
out of Bombay and out of India as soon as that
was practicable:

🌿🌿🌿
🌿🌿🌿
🌿🌿🌿

22 March, 1941

11 Temple Road
Lahore, Punjab

MY DEAR MR. RAS MOHUN,
As we have discussed before, I would like Vedi to go
to the West, where I received some of my education. I have
been worried about the child's health, and I'm sure it will
improve in the cooler, Western climate. We Punjabis thrive
in it. I'm also sure Vedi would benefit by living in a society
where people have a much more enlightened attitude toward blindness than we Indians do.

Mr. Ras Mohun had written to the Reverend Dr.
Gabriel Farrell, the director of the Perkins Institution,
in the United States, which Mr. Ras Mohun used to
refer to as "the Eton of the blind."

April 19, 1941

As from
Dadar School for the Blind,
Dadar, Bombay, (India)

DEAR DR. FARRELL,
I am writing this letter on a very important problem re-
garding the future of a bright visually handicapped boy of

157

whom I wrote to you some time ago for a Hall Braillewriter.
[Thanks to Mr. Ras Mohun, I had become the proud first
owner in India of a Hall Braillewriter, the latest American
machine for the blind. It had seven keys—six for embossing
dots and a bar for spacing—and on it I could write Braille
faster even than Deoji, who had to use a stylus and slate.]
This little fellow is doing well, and before I make a definite
request to you on his behalf, I am giving below his particu-
lars:

Pupil's Name . . . Ved Parkash Mehta

Date of birth . . . March 21, 1934

Admitted into our School . . . February, 1939

Health . . . Very good

Height . . . 3′11″

Weight . . . 49 lbs

Appearance . . . Handsome

Colour . . . Brown (almost like the Italians or Greeks)

Father's name . . . Dr. A. R. Mehta, M.B., B.S.; D.P.H.;
D.T.M. & H.; Visited Johns Hopkins School of Medicine
as a Rockefeller Foundation Fellow

Father's Profession . . . Public Health Service in the Government of the Punjab, India.

The boy has been in the school for about a year only, as
he had to be at home for another year owing to certain private family circumstances. We do not have standardized
mental tests to give to the child, but based on his responses
and my observations during the period he has been with us,
I have a feeling that probably he is a superior child. He is
very much interested in physical activities as well. He is
from a cultured family which has a tradition behind it. For
a child of his physical and mental calibre, I should like to
see that he gets an opportunity to be educated in the best
institution in the world for the visually handicapped in his
formative and most impressionable years. His father is a
very highly educated man who won scholarships in his day

and educated himself abroad mostly by self-help. He chose our school at Bombay though 1300 miles away from home because he thought that the child would have the best opportunities of education in India—such as they are. But my feeling is that a boy of such superior mentality and activity should be given the best opportunities in the world, if possible. We are teaching him through the mediums of English and the Indian vernacular of Marathi. He understands English and can write on the Hall Braillewriter. When he joined the school, he did not know a word of English. Now he has a workable vocabulary of more than 200 words. His other achievements too are remarkable.

I am, therefore, writing this letter to make a request to you, whether you could kindly make it possible to give him an opportunity of education at the Perkins Institution for the whole of his schooling period. I know the per capita cost per month last year at Perkins was 107 dollars. It may probably have a slight increase this year due to war conditions. The parents of the pupil are spending about 40 rupees per month on him. They have five other children to educate but they are so interested in the welfare of this child that I believe they may be prevailed upon and tempted to increase it up to 100 rupees (i.e. about 30 dollars according to the present exchange rates).

If you would kindly accede to my request, I shall remain grateful for two reasons. First, you would give a chance to a clever boy who would have the opportunity of being educated in the best Institution in the world and so help him diffuse your ideas of education in his province in general and his city of nearly ¾ of a million people in particular, which are extremely backward as far as the work and education of the blind is concerned. Second, he will have a much brighter future if educated at Perkins than if he were educated at any other institution in the world.

Due to war conditions the mails are so delayed that I

am sending this letter by Air Mail, so that it may reach you before you break up for summer in June. If I hear favourably from you, I can get in touch with the parents of the boy, who I am sure will agree to my plans and suggestions, if their finances permit. I feel sure that his father will never do less than his best in the matters relative to the welfare of the boy. If all our plans materialise, I would like to send the boy to America in July 1942 when Mr. and Mrs. Thomas' furlough will be due.

I shall deeply appreciate if you would kindly consider my request.

With reminiscences of Perkins and kind regards to you,

Sincerely yours,

Ras Mohun

The Rev. Dr. Gabriel Farrell, B.SC., B.D., D.D.
The Director, Perkins Institution
Watertown, Mass., U.S.A.

A couple of months later, Mr. Ras Mohun received a reply from Dr. Farrell:

June 4, 1941

The Perkins Institution
Watertown, Massachusetts

Dear Mr. Ras Mohun,

Many thanks for your letter of April 19, 1941.

I like the sound of the little fellow, but I cannot be very encouraging. I say this because I question whether a boy of his age ought to come so far from home, when it would be necessary to stay here for ten to twelve years just to graduate from our high school. It is our experience that it is better for any boy from another country not to remain here more than two years, and I suggest that he somehow carry his education to a point where he could come here for two years and be able to benefit from his experience at Perkins.

As you know, blindness is a form of maladjustment in itself, and uprooting him at this age will create many additional adjustment problems later on. His leaving home at this stage, therefore, is most inadvisable.

With my best wishes,

Cordially yours,

Gabriel Farrell

Mr. Ras Mohun and Daddyji wrote in turn to Dr. Farrell, pleading my special circumstances, but Dr. Farrell was adamant.

As a child, I knew little about all this correspondence, nor did I understand what Mr. Ras Mohun meant by "the Eton of the blind" (the poet's "distant spires" and "antique towers"). What I did know—and used to go around repeating in the boys' dormitory— was that Daddyji was planning to send me across the seas, oceans, and deserts to a big school. "There only white sahibs and memsahibs who speak English go," I used to say. "They go around in big gum boots and in big fur coats and big fur hats, because the school is covered with snow day and night." No one in the boys' dormitory would believe that there could be white sahibs and memsahibs who were blind, and the boys asked me to write to them on my Hall Braillewriter when I got there and tell them if it was really so.

X I

FIRE ON
MY HEAD

E VEN MORE THAN DURING THE FIRST YEAR AT school, I seemed to be always coming down with one sickness or another. I had sties, boils, and bronchitis—one after another. I had typhoid twice, malaria three times, and several undiagnosed diseases. In fact, I started spending as much time in the general ward of the J. J. Hospital as I did in the boys' dormitory. During my stays in the hospital, I remember, I would wake up again and again and hear a familiar footstep and say, "Daddyji has come," or I would hear a familiar rustle of a sari and say, "It's Mamaji." But there was never any Daddyji or Mamaji. (If my parents knew about my being in the hospital at all, it was after I had got better and was back at school.) There was only one doctor after another, one nurse after another. The doctors seemed always to be hurrying away, but the nurses seemed always to be waking me and giving me bitter medicine, or noisily wheeling a screen across the floor and putting it around my bed, and then changing my clothing with their cold hands or sponging me with an abrasive cloth or bringing me a bedpan.

I have forgotten everyone in the hospital except Nurse. They were all named Nurse, but one who was named Nurse was different. I would hear her sandals jauntily stepping toward my bed. She was always quietly humming some tune or other, and there was a scent of jasmine in her hair and on her clothes, which, though faint, seemed to defy the germicidal air. "I

can't swallow. My throat hurts," I would cry. I felt
I could complain to her all I wanted, in a way I felt I
couldn't to anyone else, at the hospital or at school.
"Oh, that's terrible," she would say. "Nothing could be
worse. Now, you take this throat medicine, and you'll
be all better by lunchtime. Be sure to breathe through
your nose when you sleep. That way, the medicine will
keep on working on your throat." Nurse would sit by
my bed and put her hand on my forehead to feel
whether my fever was going down, exactly as Mamaji
did. She had a small, restless hand, which was like
Mamaji's except that it had no rings on it. I would cry
if Nurse took her hand off my forehead, so she would
leave it there for long stretches. Sometimes I would fall
asleep and wake up and her hand would still be on my
forehead. I was convinced that as long as her hand was
on my forehead my temperature would stay down, and
I hated having my temperature go up, because that
made me feel as if things were going round and round
in my head.

Once, I woke up hot, feverish, and dizzy, and her
hand was gone and she was nowhere. I called for her.
Then I heard her sandals and smelled her scent and
felt her small hand on my forehead.

"You forget that I have other patients," she said.

"No. I am your only patient." I clung to her and
wept.

I made her sit by my bed and keep her hand on my
forehead.

"Why isn't Mamaji here?" I asked.

"Is she in Bombay? How many brothers and sisters
do you have?"

"One big brother, three big sisters, and one baby sister."

"Are they Christian?"

"No. Hindu. Are you a Hindu?"

"No. I am a Christian."

"Deoji is a Christian, and Uncle and Auntie are Christian. I don't know why I am a Hindu."

"You can become a Christian."

"How?"

"By praying to Jesus."

"What will happen to me when I become a Christian? Will I get well?"

"Yes, you will. You'll also go to Heaven."

"What do Christians do?"

"They look after the sick, like Jesus. A Christian tries to be good. A Christian prays to Jesus."

"I pray to Jesus, and to Mary and Joseph, but I am naughty."

"I will pray to Jesus to make you a good boy."

"When will I become a good boy?"

"When you become a good Christian."

I decided there and then to become a good Christian, and told her so.

"What do you know about Jesus?" she asked.

"In school, Uncle read with me a story about Jesus, Mary, and Joseph. They were a happy family."

"Very happy. And Jesus especially liked blind children. I'll tell you how Jesus was born. An angel came to Joseph in a dream and said that he would have a son, and the son would be the Son of God, and the son would save people from their sins."

"Things are going round and round in my head."

She pressed her hand down on my forehead. "There, they'll stop," she said. "Jesus was born in a stable in Bethlehem. Wise men came and said they had seen the star in the sky telling of his birth and they had come to worship him."

"I feel sick."

"But if you believe in him, he'll not only make you better but will open your eyes and make you see."

I became excited. "Mamaji wants me to see! I believe in him."

She asked me to repeat after her, "Heavenly Father, Thou wilt hear me."

"Heavenly Father, Thou wilt hear me."

"Bless Thy loving child tonight."

"Bless Thy loving child tonight."

"Through the darkness be Thou near me."

"Through the darkness be Thou near me."

"Keep me safe till morning light."

"Keep me safe till morning light."

"All this day Thy hand hath led me."

"All this day Thy hand hath led me."

"And I thank Thee for Thy care."

"And I thank Thee for Thy care."

"Thou hast clothed me, warmed me, fed me."

"Thou hast clothed me, warmed me, fed me."

"Listen to my evening prayer."

"Listen to my evening prayer."

"Let my sins be all forgiven."

"Let my sins be all forgiven."

"Bless the friends I love so well."

"Bless the friends I love so well."

"Take us all at last to Heaven."

"Take us all at last to Heaven."

"Happy there with Thee to dwell."

"Happy there with Thee to dwell."

"If you say this evening prayer every night and ask for your eyes back, and ask for anything else you want, Jesus will listen to you. He can comfort you more than all the nurses."

Suddenly, my forehead felt cold and exposed. Her hand was gone, and she was gone. But after that, in or out of the hospital, I never failed to say my evening prayer and ask God for all the things I wanted: for Nurse, so that I wouldn't get circles in my head; for the opening of my eyes, which would make Nurse and Mamaji happy; for glucose biscuits and soft-boiled eggs, which I could no longer have, because of the war; for an extra cigarette tin, so that I could have a separate ear-piece for my toy telephone; for thin cheeks, so that the boys wouldn't be constantly pulling my fat ones; for rough, callused hands like Abdul's, so that he could not tease me about my soft hands; for a pair of shoes for Deoji.

ABOUT THE TIME I started saying my evening prayer, I started getting circles on the outside of my head. I would wake up in the morning in the boys' dormitory and under the hair there would be a new itching spot—a circle of rough skin that would burn and sometimes swell up into a boil. I begged to see Nurse again, but Mrs. Ras Mohun said, "Everyone in the hospital is called Nurse or Doctor. There is no way of finding your nurse. Anyway, nurses only look after the very sick. You have no temperature."

"But my head itches. It's on fire."

"You have a common children's infection called ringworm," she said. "It will go away."

Mrs. Ras Mohun told the Sighted Master to see to it that my head was washed every day with Lifebuoy soap and borax, and told me not to go near Heea until the infection had cleared up. But no matter how often my head was washed I kept finding new circles on my head, until it was covered with little chains of itching, burning circles. I would scratch one part of my head and it would stop itching and burning for a while, only to set off itching and burning on another part.

"If you don't stop scratching, you'll never get better," Mrs. Ras Mohun said.

But, try as I might to stop scratching, my hands would fly up to my head, whether or not I was in front of Mr. and Mrs. Ras Mohun.

So Daddyji and Mamaji remember that when I went home for my Christmas holidays I looked so pulled down that on first seeing me at the Lahore station they almost didn't recognize me. They knew that children who went to boarding school always came back looking pulled down, but they felt that they had never seen a boarding-school child look as pulled down as I did. They had expected me to outgrow my clothes, but instead my shirt and knickers hung on me loosely. Then they noticed that I was constantly scratching my head, and that my head was covered with blisters and grayish patches.

Mamaji recalled then that when I came home for

my first Christmas holidays I had been intermittently scratching my head. She had noticed grayish-white overlapping spots on the sides and back of my head, and as she turned and flipped her fingers through my locks, tugging now at this bit of hair, now at that bit of skin, touching the sores and patches, I had cringed under her hands. She had felt proud that none of her children had ever had a single case of lice or infection on the head, so, that first Christmas, she had been dismayed. She had not known what the infection was, but when she pointed it out to Daddyji he had immediately diagnosed it as ringworm and told her to apply two-percent salicylic ointment daily. This she had done, calling it "silly sick." She and I had both made light of the infection, referring to it as "the silly sick itch."

By the time I went back to school, the silly sick itch had mostly cleared up. Daddyji had given me a letter to Mr. Ras Mohun in which he told him to apply the ointment to my head once or twice a day for a time, to keep my hair cropped, and to have my clothes, bedsheets, and pillowcases washed separately from those of the other boys. Mr. Ras Mohun had done as Daddyji told him, except that in time he had let my hair grow back. "I could easily give an order that the hair of all the blind boys in my charge be cropped," he had written to Daddyji. "That would certainly make it easier for the Sighted Master to keep the boys' heads clean and for the boys to take care of their heads. It may be that in that case we would not have instances of ringworm. But I happen to believe that it is good for the self-esteem of blind boys to feel that they have the same kind of haircut as sighted boys who, for instance, run

with them at the racing track. I think it is very important for blind boys to learn how to keep their hair clean,
how to comb it, how to part it."

I had completely forgotten about the silly sick
itch—the boys at school were always scratching their
heads.

"It's the old ringworm, all right," Daddyji now
said to Mamaji at the Lahore station. "It's come back
with a vengeance. When ringworm appears on parts of
the body without hair, it clears up very quickly. But it
looks as though the fungus had attached itself to the
roots of Vedi's hair and become stubborn. It looks as
though Vedi had been infected and reinfected by other
children at the school."

Daddyji immediately took me to the best skin specialist in Lahore. "When ringworm reaches such a stage,
it becomes resistant to any ordinary treatment," the
skin specialist said, and he recommended a treatment
for ringworm so new that even Daddyji had barely
heard of it—doses of X rays controlled in such a way
that all parts of the head would be exposed equally to
the radiation and all the hair would thereby be removed
by the roots, and the fungus with it. "I know it's a dras-
tic step," the skin specialist said. "There is a danger that
your son may be bald for the rest of his life. There is
also a small risk that it could affect his mind. But it's
the only step that offers hope now."

I didn't understand any of the discussion, but that
evening when I was helping Sher Singh make biscuits
in the kitchen he would now and then click his tongue
and shake his head; the way I knew he was shaking
his head was that he was squatting in front of the oven

but was clicking his tongue now from the left side and now from the right.

I asked him repeatedly what was wrong, but he wouldn't answer. Finally, he said, "Sahib knows what X rays are?"

"No. What are they?"

"You could say they're tongues of flame which bloodlessly enter your body and burn up anything they touch. Tomorrow, the doctors are going to burn off your hair, Sahib."

I was scared but wanted to hear more. "With a match?" I asked.

"No, much worse. With X-ray electricity. You know, the doctors burned off Anand's neck with the same electricity, and he died. If Sahib doesn't believe me, he can ask Big Sahib, but don't say I told you to."

Anand had been my baby brother. He was born and died within three months while I was in my first year at school. I had heard about him during my first Christmas holidays but hadn't been able to get anyone to tell me much about him. That night, after Sher Singh had cleared the table and gone away, I asked Daddyji, "How did Anand die?"

"He died of X-ray radiation," Daddyji said. "His thyroid was badly burned. The thyroid is a little pocket in your neck."

"How did his neck catch fire?" I asked.

There was a sudden hush at the table, broken by the clink and rattle of Mamaji's gold bangles.

"Mamaji's talking with her hands again, Daddy!" I cried. "I can hear her bangles. You've told her never to do it, and she's doing it again."

"You shouldn't do that," he said to her. "Vedi always knows, and you know how upset he gets."

Then he turned to me. "You know how your dear mother gets asthmatic attacks sometimes, when she has trouble breathing and talking, and coughs a lot. A friend of hers used to get similar attacks, and this friend was helped by X-ray treatment. The treatment was so new that it was available only in a hospital in Delhi, but, as it happened, at the time we were living in Karnal, which is just seventy-five miles from Delhi, so we eagerly availed ourselves of it. I used to drive your dear mother to Delhi for the treatment every second week. I told the X-ray specialist that your mother was carrying, but he assured me that the baby was well away from the part—what we doctors call the suprarenal gland— that was being exposed to the X rays."

I wanted to know more, but the mention of "carrying" made me shy. Shyness crawled all over me like a thousand ants, because Abdul had told me that the reason we weren't allowed to play with the girls was that if I, for instance, kissed Paran on the mouth everyone would come to know of it in a few months, because Paran would start carrying a baby, which she would cough up with her spit. "Sometimes even thinking about kissing can do it," he had said. I felt so ashamed of the knowledge that that very evening when I said Nurse's prayer I asked Jesus to make me forget it. I now secretly wished that the skin specialist would somehow burn it up along with my sores and itchy skin and make me a good Christian child again.

❦

For the prescribed X-ray treatment, Daddyji and Mamaji took me to Dr. Mathras Das Puri.

"This is Uncle Mathras Das," Daddyji said. "He's going to make your head feel all better."

"You can watch the doses of radiation yourself," Dr. Puri said to Daddyji. "If the radiation is properly controlled, his mind should not be affected, and the hair should reappear."

"What are they going to do?" I cried out.

"Nothing," Dr. Puri said. "You won't feel anything."

Dr. Puri gave me a lollipop and made me lie down on a cold table. I remembered Nurses, with their screen, and the cold pans they had put under me, and I recoiled.

"Uncle Mathras Das won't hurt you," Daddyji said, putting his large, gentle, comforting hand on my forehead. "He is my old teacher, and he's the head of the X-Ray Department at King Edward Medical College, my old school. You might say he was my Mr. Ras Mohun once."

I howled.

"You're going to be all right," Daddyji said. "Uncle Mathras Das is just going to take away all those itchy sores."

I relaxed, but then my neck touched something cold and I jumped, remembering Anand. I thought of getting down from the table, but I was very high up. I waited, expecting two Nurses to come in, one to set my hair on fire, the other to pump me. I clenched my fists and curled my toes at the end of the table, getting ready to fight.

"Lie very still," Dr. Puri said.

I heard clicks and whirs. It sounded as if someone were locking the door very fast.

I sat up. "Let me down! Let me out!" I cried.

Within a moment, Daddyji and Mamaji had lifted me off the table.

"There, there, it's all finished," they said.

"What's finished?" I asked, between my cries.

"The X ray, of course," Daddyji said.

"But I still remember what Abdul told me."

"Who is Abdul?" Daddyji asked.

"What did he tell you?" Dr. Puri asked.

I stopped crying and became very quiet.

"Say 'Thank you, Uncle Mathras Das,'" Daddyji said.

No matter how much he cajoled me, I wouldn't say it—not then, and not after the next visit, or the visit after that, or the visit after that.

ONE MORNING WHEN I woke up, I felt a thick clump of hair on my pillow. Next to my ear, there was a big bald patch, which felt cold and embarrassingly naked.

I called for Daddyji. "I can't hear well!" I cried. "I'm going to be deaf, like Jaisingh!"

"I'm sure your hearing is fine," Daddyji said. "You're only imagining."

"What will happen when I lose all my hair?" I cried.

"Nothing," he said. "It will be for just a short time. Your hair will grow back."

"Now Sister Umi will call me Baldy," I cried.

"Umi will do no such thing," Daddyji said. "Besides, bald children are nice."

"Who?" I asked, getting interested.

Daddyji hesitated. "A lot of pandits are bald," he said. "Shambu Pandit is completely bald."

I felt better, and even thought my hearing had improved.

I remember that the treatment continued for many weeks.

One morning, I woke up and I had no hair anywhere on my head. My scalp felt as smooth as the palm of my hand.

Mamaji burst into tears. "I knew you would become bald. You'll never get your hair back."

I cried along with her.

One morning some time later, I noticed that there were a few patches of stubble on my head. I ran to Daddyji, to Mamaji, to Sister Pom, to Sister Nimi, to Sister Umi, to Brother Om, to little Usha, to Sher Singh, showing off my head and crying out, "See, my hair is growing back! I'm not going to be bald! I'm not going to be a bald boy!"

Years later, Daddyji told me, "Although your hair did grow back, it was not as profuse and thick as before. The hair on top of your head was especially thin. Also, the hair had receded from your forehead. The pity was that within a few years of your X-ray treatment there were anti-fungus drugs in India which could be taken by mouth and which were effective against ringworm. But these drugs had come to India too late for the treatment of your ringworm. As it happened, wonder drugs like penicillin had also come to India too late for the treatment of your meningitis."

❧

AFTER I GOT MY new hair, Mamaji began building up my health for my return to school. Every day, she would give me cups of boiled fresh milk from a cow she was keeping tethered in the *gulli* in front of our house. The mere smell of the hot milk and the touch of the skin floating on it would make me want to vomit. The skin would cling to my mouth or to the rim of the cup, no matter how I tried to avoid it. I would push the cup away, but she would make me drink the milk, sometimes adding cocoa or Ovaltine to it to make it more palatable. Mamaji would also churn butter herself and spoon it into my mouth, sometimes lacing it with peeled almonds and sugar. I wouldn't like the milky-smelling gooey blobs any more than I liked the milk, but she would make me eat the butter.

At the table, my big sisters and big brother talked about their treats at Kevanter's restaurant.

"You can get tasty flavored milk there, as cold as ice cream," Sister Umi said.

"It's wonderfully cold," Sister Pom said.

"It's strawberry milk," Sister Nimi said.

"And you drink it with straws," Brother Om said.

I got excited thinking of ice-cream-like milk tasting of strawberries and drunk with straws. But I was never taken to Kevanter's. Mamaji didn't trust restaurant milk and didn't think it particularly healthful for me. In any case, it was something that grownup children drank. At the time, Sister Pom was fifteen, Sister Nimi was fourteen, Sister Umi was twelve, and Brother Om was nearly eleven. I was then not quite eight.

When Daddyji thought that I was healthy enough, he reluctantly decided to send me back to school. "I didn't know what else to do," he says. "I was impressed by your progress and your growing independence, and I wanted you to get as much out of Dadar School as you could. I did, however, write to Mr. Ras Mohun pleading with him to segregate your clothes from the other boys' and also to write again to Dr. Farrell. I was sure Perkins would accept you on a second try. But then I am a dreamer."

XII

GROWING WHEN YOU'RE SLEEPING

A WEEK OR TWO AFTER I ARRIVED AT SCHOOL FOR MY third stay (the year was 1942), I went into the sitting-and-dining room for my breakfast singing, "Yes, we have no bananas today." At one time, Mrs. Ras Mohun used to cut up bananas over my porridge, which made the porridge taste better. But now, because of the war, there were not only no eggs and no glucose biscuits but also no bananas.

"What is that 'yes-no' nonsense?" Mrs. Ras Mohun asked, with a little laugh.

"It's a war song Daddyji heard on a ship when he was going to England for his studies," I said.

"You will have a war, all right, with Uncle, if you go on confusing yes and no."

"Yes, we have no bananas today!" I yelled.

Mrs. Ras Mohun served me my porridge and asked me to eat quietly.

MR. RAS MOHUN STARTED a new practice. Every morning, after breakfast, we all had to gather in front of his office, at the back of the workshop area, and go in, one by one, and tell him our dreams of the night before. "I am writing a book with a chapter about how the dreams of the blind differ from those of the sighted," he had explained to us. "For every dream you tell me, I will give you a sweet."

One morning, as we were waiting outside Mr. Ras

Mohun's office for our turn to go in, Miss Mary asked Rashmi, "What dream are you going to tell?" Rashmi was an eleven-year-old girl who was totally blind.

"I am going to tell my dream about my holidays," Rashmi said. "In my dream, I went home for my holidays. My mother was very angry. She asked me, 'Why did you come home? You don't belong here. You belong in the school.' 'I wanted to see you all,' I said. 'I was missing you.' I felt very sad that my mother was angry. But then Mr. Ras Mohun arrived. 'Hello, Rashmi,' he said. 'How are you? Come along, let's go back to school.' I felt very happy. 'Most gladly will I go with you,' I said. When I got back to school, all the boys and girls were sitting on the veranda and eating. I asked them, 'What are you eating?' Miss Mary, you were very angry. 'The first thing you ask us is about food? What a question!' you said. I began to cry, and I was sad all over again."

"That's a nice dream," Miss Mary said.

"But there's no blind stuff in it, Miss Mary," Abdul said. "She won't get a sweet."

Rashmi sniffled.

"But we are all in it," Miss Mary said. "Mr. Ras Mohun will like that dream. Rashmi will most certainly get a sweet. And what dream are you going to tell, Meena?"

"I am going to tell my dream about a famine," Meena said. Meena was a girl of ten. "I dreamed that we had nothing to eat. There was no rain. The grass died. Cows had nothing to eat. They died. People died. I was afraid that in school we would have no food to eat and no milk to drink. Suddenly, the rains came, and we all ran out to play in the water. Then the air got very cold. The Matron saw us outside and got very angry. 'You'll catch fever!' she shouted. We were frightened and ran back into the dormitories. Then we sowed some seeds in Mrs. Ras Mohun's flower-and-vegetable bed. First there were buds and then there were full flowers. We felt very happy because the famine was over."

All the girls said that that was a nice dream, and we all surrounded Miss Mary. "Miss Mary, Miss Mary, what dream are you going to tell?"

"I dreamed that Paran and I were threading a garland in the girls' domitory," she said. "We ran out of flowers. I went down to the garden to gather some flowers. A big snake slid over my foot. It was long and heavy. I ran. The snake came after me, hissing all the while. I called out, 'Gardener, kill the snake!' He came and killed the snake with his stick. Ahead were the Matron and all you girls, and you were laughing and laughing. 'That was no snake,' the Matron said. 'It was just a vine.'"

"What kind of flowers were they?" I asked.

"They were just flowers," Miss Mary said.

"What color?" I persisted.

"No special color—just white," she said, a bit sharply.

I remembered our little garden, in front of our house in Lahore, and felt sad. I would follow Mamaji around the garden, tugging at her sari, asking her the color of this big round flower, the name of that funnel of a flower, the reason for the smell of these crinkly leaves, and the reason for those stiff stems with thorns in them. I would squeeze a lily and a marigold and compare the saps. I would hold a petal of a sunflower up to one nostril and a petal of a queen of the night up to the other and compare the scents. I would take a bite out of a gardenia and a bite out of a rose and compare the flavors.

"Vedi." I heard Mr. Ras Mohun open the door and call my name. "Come in."

I stood on the thick, crunchy coconut matting in front of Mr. Ras Mohun's table, trying not to make noise and not to yawn. I was afraid that if I yawned I would forget my dream and wouldn't get a sweet, so I kept my mouth tightly shut, trying to hold the dream in.

"What did you dream last night?" he asked, sitting down at his table.

"I was with a doggie. He was walking about. He was white and brown. He was Bobby. I called out to him, 'Chu! Chu! Chu! Come to my bed!' He came. I asked Bobby, 'Don't you feel sleepy, doggie?' 'No,' he said. Then he barked at someone who was walking about. Deoji woke up, and said, 'Bobby, don't bark. School dogs are not supposed to bark at school boys.' Then Deoji, Bobby, and I went to sleep."

"You must remember colors from before you went blind," Mr. Ras Mohun said, picking up his pen and writing. "Anyway, you come from a cultured home."

I waited for my sweet, listening to the nib of Mr. Ras Mohun's pen screeching along the paper.

"Hold out your hand," Mr. Ras Mohun finally said. He tilted the sweet jar into my hand. I knew from other mornings that it had two kinds of sweets in it. One was like a marble with a flat bottom; it was lemonish in flavor and melted in the mouth quickly. The other was in the shape of an orange section, with indentations all around; it was long-lasting. Moreover, if I kept the orange sweet in the inside of my cheek for some time it would stamp its sugary impression there, and I could taste the orangy sweetness long after I'd finished the sweet—especially if I was careful to keep my cheek a little bit puckered. But the orange sweets had a tendency to stick in the jar. I wanted to fish one out of the jar, but I was afraid of Mr. Ras Mohun's ruler. I prayed to Jesus, Mary, and Joseph to let an orange sweet fall into my hand, but what dropped was a lemon sweet.

Mr. Ras Mohun entered Deoji in the American Marathi Mission School for sighted boys. "Our school only goes up through the fourth standard," he explained to us. "Deoji has finished the fourth standard. Deoji will be a good experiment to see if the blind can study in sighted schools."

"Mr. Ras Mohun has got his experiment from America," Abdul said. "There, if the blind study with sighted boys they eventually become sighted."

"Will Deoji become more sighted now?" I asked.

"Son of an owl! That's what happens in America, where people have big, strong eyes," Abdul said. "Anyway, that only happens to the half sighted, and lately Deoji's eyes have got really bad. He's now almost as blind as we are."

Deoji would leave early in the morning, with a

peon from his new school, who had come to fetch him, and would not return until after tiffin. When he came back, we would circle around him and ask him "What is that school like?" and "What are the sighted boys like?" and "Do you like it over there?"

But Deoji told us little. "Oh, I like it a lot better over here," he would say. "The sighted boys don't talk to me much. I am trying all the time, but they are not trying."

"To them, you are like Jaisingh," Abdul once told him. "We don't talk to him here, because he doesn't have ears, and they don't talk to you over there, because you don't have eyes."

I missed having Deoji at school all day. Every few minutes in the afternoon, I would run up to the peon at the gate and ask him, "What time is it? Has my Loving Big Brother Deoji come back?"

"Go and play," the peon would say. "He'll come in his own good time."

Sometimes I would slip away after lunch or tiffin and go and sit on Deoji's bed in the boys' dormitory and pray to Jesus, Mary, and Joseph for Deoji to start studying with us at our school again.

ONE SATURDAY, Deoji came running up to the boys' dormitory. "I was trying to get my *dilrubah* out of the classroom for practicing my music," he said breathlessly. "I put my foot on something. It felt like a quivering plantain, but I couldn't see what it was. I was so frightened."

"It was probably a dead rat," Abdul said.

I had once accidentally picked up a dead rat in the back courtyard. I thought it was a large, dried-out mango stone, because it had little brushlike hairs sticking out all around. Then I touched its curled tail. I dropped it and ran up to the boys' dormitory. "You've touched a rat," Abdul said. "Now you'll swell up all over and die of the plague." For weeks afterward, I would wake up in the middle of the night and feel myself all over, to see if I was swollen; I was sure that I would be stricken by the plague. Even now, as I thought of the dead rat, I shuddered.

"It was alive," Deoji said. "I'm certain of that."

The Sighted Master came in and wanted to know why we were all trembling.

"Deoji stepped on something live!" we cried, and we told him about it.

"A snake has got into the school," the Sighted Master said, with clenched teeth. "I've been waiting to kill a snake for a long time."

The Sighted Master started down the stairs, and we followed. He called for the peon to bring him a lantern. (There was no electricity downstairs.)

"It's a snake!" the Sighted Master cried. "Quick, peon, a stick!"

I heard the Sighted Master deliver one blow with the stick—a padded, squishy sound.

"Got it right on the head," the Sighted Master said. "It's a cobra. Must have just missed Deoji. Peon, hurry and take the cobra out and bury it, or its children will be all over the school."

There was a chattering of teeth all around.

After that, we never went downstairs after dark, and we didn't joke about snakes anymore.

❦

AT NIGHT, once we heard the Sighted Master snoring—and his snores were almost as loud as a lorry backfiring—we would start whispering to one another. Sometimes I would fall asleep and wake up and the boys would still be talking: Did Mr. and Mrs. Ras Mohun brush their teeth? Did they pick their noses? Did they rub their eyes? Did they snore? Did they go to the bathroom? Did Mr. Ras Mohun dream about lady ghosts coming into his bed? What did Mrs. Ras Mohun feel like between her shoulders? What would happen to a boy if he ran up and touched her and pretended it was an accident?

I woke up once and heard Abdul and Bhaskar having a heated discussion—practically shouting at each other in whispers.

"Mr. Ras Mohun doesn't pee-pee," Abdul was saying. "He doesn't do those dirty things. He's not blind."

"But I'm half sighted, and I pee-pee," Bhaskar said. "Mr. Ras Mohun does too pee-pee."

"You pee-pee because you're blind," Abdul said. "You're blind, or you wouldn't be in this blind school."

"I'm not blind," Bhaskar said. "You're blind. Besides, the Sighted Master pee-pees."

"But the Sighted Master doesn't speak English."

They were silent, and then suddenly Abdul asked, "Do you think *she* pee-pees?"

"Who? Mrs. Ras Mohun? No. How could she?"

I thought I heard the distant roar of Mr. Ras Mohun opening the accordion gate. No, it wasn't the accordion gate at all; it was the click-click of his shoes close by. I tried to call out to Abdul and Bhaskar and warn them, but my voice wouldn't come. My heart began to race. I tried to call out again, and my voice came in a scream. "Shoes! Mr. Ras Mohun!"

I was terrified. The boys' dormitory became still. I thought that Mr. Ras Mohun was going to descend on us at any moment with his ruler.

"What is it?" the Sighted Master muttered through his deep sleep. "Quiet . . . Mr. Ras Mohun . . ." He turned over and started snoring again, roaring and clicking like the accordion gate and Mr. Ras Mohun's shoes.

ONE NIGHT, I heard someone fumbling with my mosquito net. I lay very still. Except for Deoji and the Sighted Master, whose beds flanked mine, no one was permitted to enter the aisles next to my bed at night. In fact, by Mr. Ras Mohun's orders, no boy was allowed to enter the aisles next to any other boy's bed after the lights were out. Yet I felt sure that it wasn't Deoji, because he usually pulled out the mosquito net from the middle of the bed, and the intruder was undoing the mosquito net near my pillow. I also felt sure that it wasn't the Sighted Master, because he had never opened my mosquito net. Besides, he was roaring and clicking in his bed.

A hand reached in, caught hold of me by my shoulder, and shook me. I was wearing my pajama coat, and through the cloth I couldn't make out whose hand it was. I pretended to be asleep. "Vedi, come with me," I heard Abdul say in my ear, so softly that the words were little more than a breath.

"Why?" I said into my pillow. "What for?"

"I want to show you the ruler."

"Mr. Ras Mohun's ruler?" I was suddenly fully awake. "How did you get hold of it?"

"Quick!"

I sat up. The Sighted Master was snoring so loudly that he sounded as if he were beating a growling dog. All the boys seemed to be breathing regularly, as if their souls were having adventures far, far away.

I climbed down from my bed and followed Abdul out of the boys' dormitory.

I expected Abdul to turn left and go down the stairs and show me Mr. Ras Mohun's ruler in the front courtyard, near the forbidden window of the Muhammadan Hotel, but instead he turned right, toward the boys' common bathroom, and went in.

I hesitated at the door. The boys' common bathroom was just next to the accordion gate, and it was general knowledge that Mr. Ras Mohun slipped down occasionally and checked to make sure that there was no "boy mischief" going on there. I had heard that before I arrived at the school a couple of boys had been caught at boy mischief and had been sent away from the school, to go no one knew where. But then I couldn't wait to examine Mr. Ras Mohun's ruler. I never felt I knew a thing until I had touched it, and touched it all over, from every side. Sometimes the wish to touch a thing I had heard about, like Mr. Ras Mohun's ruler, would so agitate me that I couldn't stop thinking about it. The name of the thing would go on repeating itself in my head—"Mr. Ras Mohun's ruler, Mr. Ras Mohun's ruler"—like a permanently stuck record. Of course, I had an impression of Mr. Ras Mohun's ruler, from the time he had rested it against my arm threateningly during the making of "Darkness," but I had no idea whether it was thin or thick; whether it was tall, like a bamboo pole, or short, like a swagger stick; whether it was natural and knotted or polished and smooth. I went into the boys' common bathroom.

The floor was wet and slippery. A wasp buzzed in one corner, the pitch of his buzz rising and falling as if he were calling to another wasp. The bathroom ghost, as watchful as the Sighted Master, turned his head in our direction, creaking his neck. The place felt close and smelled dirty. I choked and coughed.

"Sh-h-h!" Abdul said. "You will wake up Mr. Ras Mohun. Give me your hand."

I held out my hand. I expected him to let me feel Mr. Ras Mohun's ruler. But he grabbed my hand in his rough one and pulled it down the slope of his belly. I resisted. He abruptly caught hold of my forefinger and stuck it into a hole in the middle of his belly.

I was excited. I had never felt anyone else's navel before, and it felt deeper and more snug than mine. But I screamed—I was surprised by the sound of my own voice.

Abdul clamped his free hand over my mouth. I slipped and fell on my knees.

The door swung open, and I heard Mr. Ras Mohun's falsetto. "Boy mischief. Vedi, what was your finger doing there?" I felt Mr. Ras Mohun's eyes burn through my finger.

Mr. Ras Mohun propelled me out the door. I heard a terrible thud and Abdul's cracked scream.

I waited in my bed for Mr. Ras Mohun's ruler—my arms, my back, and my stomach tingling in anticipation of the blow, even as I tried to shut out the rising hubbub in the boys' dormitory:

"Boy mischief!"

"Boy mischief?"

"Who?"

"Abdul and Vedi."

"Vedi!"

I don't remember ever hearing Abdul return to his bed; I don't remember falling asleep or waking up. But I remember that the next morning the boys avoided me, as they had the time I wouldn't eat bitter gourd. I also remember that when I went into the sitting-and-dining room—Mr. Ras Mohun forced me to go in—I felt Mr. Ras Mohun's eyes again burn through my finger. Later, I washed my finger again and again with Lifebuoy soap and cold water and rubbed it, but it wouldn't feel clean, and the burning wouldn't go away.

I waited for Abdul to be sent away from the school and for Daddyji to send for me—I was certain Mr. Ras Mohun had written to him. But days went by and nothing happened to either of us. I tried to keep my dirty, burning finger in my pocket whenever I could.

❧

THERE WERE TWO adjacent beds in the boys' dormitory which we had dubbed Eenie and Meenie after we learned the English ditty from Mr. Ras Mohun. The Eenie bed belonged to Jaisingh, the Meenie bed to Ramesh.

Ramesh was two years older than I was, but he was smaller than I was. He spoke as if he had clusters of sweets inside his cheeks, and he dragged his feet and always walked in a crooked line. He seemed to be all bones and no skin. Whenever he went to bed, he cried, as if the wooden planks pained his body. I remember that I once told Mrs. Ras Mohun he should have a soft bed, like mine, and she said, "He's not a special student from a cultured home." Ramesh was slow in classes; everything had to be explained to him several times. He was also touchy; if anyone pulled his shirt, he got badly upset. But he didn't know how to fight back, so the boys were constantly going up to him and pulling his shirt.

Jaisingh sounded like a big boy and had fuzz on his cheeks, though he was only four years older than I was. He could neither hear nor see, and could speak very little. He had come to our school straight from the hospital, at the age of four, and for the next three years he was so sick that Mr. Ras Mohun let him stay in bed all the time and excused him from all the classes. Then Mr. Ras Mohun got an audit-tube, a sort of horn, and while Jaisingh touched Mr. Ras Mohun's throat Mr. Ras Mohun shouted through the tube into Jaisingh's ear. He found that Jaisingh could hear a little after all. After that, Mr. Ras Mohun came regularly to the boys' dormitory and gave Jaisingh a talking-class in his bed. Jaisingh slowly learned to follow a few commands and recognize a few objects. Mr. Ras Mohun used to call him the Dadar School's Helen Keller. We didn't know who Helen Keller was, but we imagined that she was an American Jaisingh. Jaisingh had to be helped everywhere. Two or three times a day, the Sighted Master took him out to the back courtyard, and Jaisingh showed great interest in going up the climbing bars and jumping down. As he hit the ground, he would laugh uncontrollably. If we happened to be playing in the back courtyard, too, and one of us tried to take a turn at the climbing bars, Jaisingh would shriek.

Jaisingh couldn't even go to the bathroom by himself; in fact, he couldn't even say "small bathroom" or "big bathroom." When he was trying to be a good boy, he would make noises as if he wanted to go to the bathroom. He would grunt and bleat, and then the Sighted Master would run to him and take him to the boys' common bathroom. But sometimes in the night he would do his small bathroom and big bathroom in bed, and then, instead of being sorry about it, he would let out a howl. The howl was so loud that it would wake up the Sighted Master. The Sighted Master would run to him, and when he found out what Jaisingh had done he would beat him, with an old, discarded shoe of Mr. Ras Mohun's that the Sighted Master kept under his bed. "Why didn't you make your bathroom noises?" he would shout, forgetting that Jaisingh couldn't hear him. Often, Jaisingh had made those noises and the Sighted Master had slept through them, but Jaisingh would be beaten anyway. We never dared to tell the Sighted Master that Jaisingh had made the noises, no matter how much we wanted to, because if any of us talked back—or even cried—we would be beaten, too. So whenever we heard poor Jaisingh being beaten we would feel sad.

Some of us who were totally blind had been sighted once, but we could no longer remember what that was like. We thought of sighted people as awesome and powerful, always able to take a discarded shoe to someone who wasn't sighted. For when we thought of being sighted, we could think of ourselves only as the Sighted Master, never as Mr. Ras Mohun upstairs, never as the peon at the gate, never as a parent at home or a missionary parent at a foundling home. This was perhaps because the Sighted Master slept in the boys' dormitory and therefore, in a sense, was one of us, or perhaps because the Sighted Master had a discarded shoe that was almost always sitting under his bed, where we could go and feel it, or perhaps simply because of the name Sighted Master. We would dream of growing up and becoming the Sighted Master—living in the boys' dormitory, snoring away, catching boys doing naughty things, beating them with a discarded shoe—even as we would automatically straighten ourselves at the very mention of the Sighted Master.

Ramesh and Jaisingh would cry in the middle of the night. The Sighted Master would shout from his bed "Stop it!" and Ramesh would generally stop, but Jaisingh would go on crying until the Sighted Master got up and took the shoe to him. Actually, we got so used to Jaisingh's crying, to his eerie moans and wails, that we were aware of the sounds only when they suddenly stopped.

One night, both Ramesh and Jaisingh began crying, and neither would stop. I heard the Sighted Master
curse and get up. I waited for the scraping sound that I
always heard when he was fumbling around for the
shoe, but I didn't hear it. "The blind devils!" he muttered. "I would rather break stones, but there are no
jobs to be had. The damned blind devils."

He stubbed his toe on the foot of my long bed and
cursed some more.

I heard him walk slowly, in his bare feet, to Jaisingh's bed. "I will finish Ras Mohun's Helen Keller,"
he said.

Two beds over from Jaisingh's, Bhaskar was snoring slightly. On the other side of Bhaskar, Abdul was
grinding his teeth.

I heard the Sighted Master struggling with a bed
plank. The plank slipped off the iron frame and bounced
on the floor like the end of a seesaw. I knew that it was
a plank from either Ramesh's or Jaisingh's bed, but I
couldn't tell which, because I wasn't sure exactly where
the Sighted Master was. I heard the plank banging and
reverberating on the floor and against the iron frame.
All at once, Bhaskar stopped snoring and Abdul stopped
grinding his teeth. I curled up at the bottom of my bed,
trying to make myself as small as I could, and breathed
as silently as I could. I repeated to myself, "Heavenly
Father, Thou wilt hear me." Then Ramesh stopped crying. I thought that Jaisingh would also decide to be a
good boy, and that the Sighted Master would go back
to his bed. But Jaisingh continued crying.

Then I heard a swishing noise that reminded me of

Sher Singh raising an axe to chop a piece of wood. After that, I heard a sound that was hard to remember later. It could have been like the swatting of a fly or the slam of a screen door or the beating of a coat with a coat brush. But it was very penetrating. Jaisingh's crying abruptly stopped, and everything became completely still. Then there was the clatter of the plank being replaced on the iron frame.

The Sighted Master started walking back toward his bed. I thought he paused for a second at the foot of my bed, but then I heard him hurrying on and fumbling to get back into his own bed.

I stayed awake for a long time, waiting to hear a sound from Jaisingh. Finally, I thought I heard him begin to moan in a sustained manner, like the motor of an old car that won't start. I immediately fell asleep.

The next day, when I came back from having breakfast with Mr. and Mrs. Ras Mohun the boys were whispering about Ramesh and Jaisingh.

"Their beds are empty," Abdul said. "They're gone."

I went over and felt all around Ramesh's and Jaisingh's beds. The thin sheets that had covered them had been removed, but all the planks were intact—they felt dry, like kindling wood.

"He killed them last night," Abdul said. "Both of them. The Sighted Master did, with two blows of a plank."

"There was only one blow," Reuben said.

"I heard Jaisingh cry afterward," I said.

"No, you didn't," Abdul said. "You were dreaming. The Sighted Master took a plank off the bed and cracked first one head and then the other. I heard it with my own ears."

"No, he didn't kill Ramesh," Bhaskar said. "I saw it with my good eye. He killed Jaisingh."

"No, I think Jaisingh has gone off to a new, deaf-and-dumb school," Tarak Nath said.

"Good riddance of bad rubbish," Abdul said.

"They didn't die," Reuben said. "I think they have been taken to the hospital for throat operations."

"Eenie, meenie, miney mo," Abdul chanted, jumping on and off Jaisingh's bed. "Catch a tiger by the toe. If he hollers, let him go."

We were confused about precisely what had happened that night, and some of us waited for Ramesh or Jaisingh—or both—to come back. But neither of them came back, and in due course their beds were given to two new boys.

I wanted to ask Mr. Ras Mohun what had happened to Ramesh and Jaisingh, but I was afraid of the Sighted Master.

❧

ONE DAY WHEN we came up from our game period, we found a pussycat in the boys' dormitory. No one knew how she had got there or what she was doing there, but we were all excited, and we all gathered around her, trying to touch her, pat her, hold her. She was a fluffy little thing. Her long tail pointed almost straight up, and she waved her paws as we passed her from hand to hand. We all remarked how different she felt from the hard, lumpy cloth kitten in the birds-and-animals class.

Abdul took charge of the pussycat. Every morning and evening, he would bring up from his meals a little milk in a clay saucer and give it to her with a piece of maize bread. He made sure she was comfortable at night under a bed. Each of us got a chance to keep the pussycat under his bed one time or another, and we became fond of her.

One morning, as Abdul was picking the pussycat up from under his bed, she scratched his face, and he announced, "I have lost my fondness for the pussycat." I didn't like her anymore, either.

The reason I remember the day the pussycat scratched Abdul is that when we went down for our morning class afterward Mr. Ras Mohun was there. He hushed us all, and said, "Boys and girls, this is a bad day for us. The German enemy today has invaded yet another country. Japanese bombing of Bombay can't be ruled out. The government has said that from now on there are going to be regular air-raid drills. Whenever you hear the bugle, you are all to run down to the tunnel—the old, unused sewer—under the cellar, and you are not to come out until I personally call you. I am appointing Reuben and Tarak Nath your prefects. It will be their responsibility to move the stone from the mouth of the tunnel and then push it back after they have made sure that everyone is inside. They are strong fellows and should be able to manage the stone."

That night, the Marathi broadcast on the radio said, "Many Indians want the Germans and Japanese to win, because these Indians think they will liberate us from the British, but do they know about the Germans' policy of killing the weaklings? The Germans will shoot dead the well-to-do, with their soft hands; the poor, with their sick bodies; and also the blind, the deaf, and the dumb. They have use only for able-bodied people who can fight. And the Japanese are no better than the Germans. So, brothers and sisters, let us all fight to keep the German raj from coming to the shores of India."

We were all frightened, because we imagined that if the Germans came to India we at the school would be the first ones to be killed.

A few days later, we heard the roar of airplanes and the whine and scream of the air-alert bugle. We were in our morning class. We fell over each other running down to the tunnel to hide.

"The Germans are coming to kill us!" Meena screamed over and over. Miss Mary tried to shush her, but Meena wouldn't stop screaming.

Just as we started sliding down the tunnel entrance, Mr. Ras Mohun came and announced, "The air raid is over for today. You can go back to your class."

Later that day, when we were up in the boys' dormitory, I told Abdul about Ajmero, and how she had died. "I wonder what being dead feels like," I said to him. "I wonder what we'll feel like when we die. Like a dead rat?"

"If you like, I will show you exactly what it's like this evening, in the back courtyard," he said.

"No boy mischief," I said. "Mr. Ras Mohun will send you away, and the Germans will kill you."

"Boy mischief!" Abdul exclaimed. "Never again in my life!"

After dinner, he and I slipped downstairs to the back courtyard. There was a little stirring in the close air, as if we had startled the ghosts.

"I think I don't want to know about death," I said.

"Feel what I've got here in my arms."

"Boy mischief!" I cried.

"Never again in my life, I told you!" Abdul said.

I reached out cautiously and felt his arms. He was cradling something soft, furry, and a little wet. I recoiled.

"It's only the pussycat," he said. "I've just bathed her to get her ready for your death lesson."

"What are you going to do?"

"I'm going to put her underground, like a potato. I'm going to bury her."

"But she's not dead."

"I know. But her time has come."

"I'm going back upstairs," I said.

"Don't you want to know what death feels like? Don't you remember how she scratched me? A bite from a mad animal can kill you just as quickly as a German gun."

"What will happen when we put her underground?" I asked.

"You wait and see. She'll feel very different. She'll feel like death."

I got interested and forgot all about ghosts and sleep, about boy mischief and my earlier fondness for the pussycat. Under Abdul's direction, I got an old garden bucket that was standing nearby. It had some water in it, and we used the water to moisten a little patch of Mrs. Ras Mohun's flower-and-vegetable bed. At that spot, we then dug a big hole. Abdul put the pussycat in the hole. I suddenly thought of the pussycat in a new way: she was like a little piece of potato that would grow into a plant if it was watered regularly.

The pussycat seemed sleepy and tired, but she began meowing and scratching, trying to climb out of the hole. I was afraid we were going to be discovered, and I was about to run back upstairs. Then Abdul slammed the bucket over her and sat on it.

"That's the last time she will scratch anyone," he said.

"But she's clawing and meowing in there," I said. "She's going to bite you. She's going to kill you."

"Quick!" Abdul said. "Help me fill the hole."

We filled the hole and made the ground level. Immediately, it was all still in the back courtyard. The pussycat and the bucket had disappeared, as if they had never been.

We raced upstairs to the boys' dormitory. "If anyone asks you about the pussycat, tell them that she ran away during the air raid," Abdul said.

I don't know what I'd expected, but when Abdul and I went to the burial spot a couple of nights later I was shocked. It was all dry and crumbly, as if the bucket had been a heaving oven, and when we dug up the pussycat she was stiff and bent and bony, her fluff turned into a brushy mat, and her claws fallen off. She had only clumps for feet.

"We will be turned out of the school if anyone

finds out about the pussycat," Abdul said, throwing her in the school rubbish bin.

I think it was around that time—but it could have been much later, because the air-raid drills at the school soon became as regular as classes—that I had a dream and I went to Mr. Ras Mohun to tell it to him.

"Another dream about going across seas, oceans, and deserts to America?" he asked.

"No, Uncle. It's about the Germans. They came to the school as Bhaskar and I were going into the class-room. The Germans shouted and said something to us angrily. We were frightened and ran upstairs to the boys' dormitory. The Germans followed us. They stayed with us in the boys' dormitory for three days. We gave them food and water. Then they called all of us—boys and girls—together on the veranda and asked us, 'Who are your prefects and group leaders?' We would not tell them. They went into a rage. Somehow they found out and killed the prefects."

"And how did you know that your Germans killed them?"

"Uncle, they made a lot of noise. I heard the clanking of their arms, and their shouts and cries, and there was wet blood all around. Then they killed all of us."

I got my sweet—an orange one.

XIII

AMONG HOMES

B ECAUSE OF THE WAR, I WENT HOME SEVERAL TIMES for extra holidays. Each time, it seemed, I went to a different place. That was because Daddyji was often transferred from one town in the Punjab to another; in fact, between the time I was three and the time I was eight he was posted, in turn, to Gujrat, to Lahore, to Karnal, to Amritsar, to Lahore, to Multan, to Ambala, to Lahore, to Rawalpindi, to Ambala, to Lahore, and to Rawalpindi. In each place, he was given a government bungalow that went with his posting. I never knew exactly why he was transferred, though during the time I was with the family I would hear Daddyji mention at the table or on the veranda that there was a *mela* (festival) planned in some place and his services were required, or that there was a promotion in the offing, or that some Muslim officer had it in for him. Anyway, I remember that in those days Daddyji and Mamaji didn't seem to be in one place for very long, and that they sent my big sisters and my big brother to boarding schools— Sisters Pom, Nimi, and Umi to the Sacred Heart Convent in Lahore (Brother Om stayed on at Bishop Cotton School, in Simla)—so that their studies would not be continually interrupted. Years later, I asked Daddyji why he did not let Mamaji stay in our house at 11 Temple Road, in Lahore, and let my big sisters and my big brother be day scholars—like some of our cousins, whose fathers were transferred from place to place but whose mothers stayed back in the city. "Either their fa-

thers didn't believe in the English system of boarding-
school education, as I did, or they couldn't afford it," he
said. "Anyway, I wanted to have your dear mother with
me, so that we could make a home wherever we went."
But often there was no home to go to during our school
holidays, and although Daddyji had kept a couple of
rooms for our use at 11 Temple Road—the house was
rented out—they were always occupied by Daddyji's
sister (our *bhua,* or paternal aunt), Parmeshwari Devi,
and her five children, my Anand cousins. They wouldn't
vacate the rooms, because, among other things, they
considered the number eleven to be lucky; the Anand
cousins seemed always to be sitting for school or job
examinations and therefore felt they needed a lot of
luck. So during our school holidays we children often
stayed with our maternal grandfather and grandmother,
Babuji and Mataji. They had a big bungalow at 16 Mozang Road, just across Temple Road and around the
corner from our house, with a lawn and lots of servants—a driver, a water carrier, a gardener, and a cook
as well as bearers and sweepers. Although 16 Mozang
Road didn't have many bedrooms, it seemed that it
could accommodate any number of beds. Babuji and
Mataji's children seemed to be constantly arriving with
their families and servants for long stays, and the bungalow had the atmosphere of a family festival.

What I liked most about staying in Mozang Road
was the daily visits of the Hakimji—a doctor who practiced the Unani system of medicine. He came every
evening, and I always knew by the sound of his shoes
that he had come. He wore loose pumps, and I imagined that because they had no laces he had to hug

them to his feet; anyway, his walk was a series of kicks and scrapes which to us had a princely sound. Whenever we children heard Hakimji's footsteps on the veranda, we would all run out to him and stand with our wrists outstretched.

"Feel my pulse first, Hakimji!"

"Take my pulse first, Hakimji!"

"No, my pulse, Hakimji!"

One by one, he would take our wrists, feel our pulse, and give us *churan* (powder) wrapped in pieces of old newspaper. The *churan* tasted of honey and ground pepper but had the consistency of salt. We liked to eat our fill of *churan,* until our breath smelled of it— a condition that Hakimji assured us was a sign of lively health. If we had an itchy spot, a bleeding injury, or aches and pains, he would also give us dabs of heavy Green Ointment in small Pond's-cold-cream jars. We would apply the Green Ointment and wait for relief.

"The fellow is a quack," Daddyji would say. "He's no doctor—he's a medicine man. People like him should be behind bars. They do more harm than good."

When we were with Daddyji, we believed him. But when Hakimji was taking our pulse with his princely fingers or giving us his Green Ointment we believed Mamaji, who said he was the greatest doctor in Lahore. All the Mehras—Mamaji's side of the family— believed in him, and at 16 Mozang Road he had the privileges of a great doctor. He was free to walk through the house unannounced, and was the only man who was free to enter the women's quarters there without knocking.

At one time, I hadn't liked Hakimji, but that was

before I was introduced to his *churan* and his Green Ointment. Right after I went blind, I was moved from the hospital to Mozang Road. It was there that Mamaji would catch hold of me and put stinging drops in my eyes. When I cried out, she would say, "It's Hakimji's medicine. There, there, the stinging will go away. Hakimji says the drops will make you see." After a while, when I needed something, like being taken to the bathroom, I stopped calling Mamaji. Instead, I would call Ajmero. If she was not within earshot, I would call Mamaji's next-younger sister, Auntie Dharam. Auntie Dharam would come running. Then she got married and went away. After that, I would call Mamaji's second sister, Auntie Pushpa—until the orange-sweets incident, that is.

Auntie Pushpa was sitting in front of her dressing table. I smelled orange sweets and ran up to her. "May I have some?" I asked.

"Go away," she said. "You're a big nuisance." Her head was bent down, and she was doing something to some orange sweets with her hands.

"What are you doing to the orange sweets?" I asked, trying to climb up onto her lap. "Let me feel."

She put something on the back of my hand with a brush. I smelled the back of my hand and knew what she was doing—she was making orange-sweets syrup. I reached across to the dressing table and picked up a little bottle. It smelled of orange-sweets syrup. I started to drink it up. I choked.

"Look out!" she cried. "You're drinking my fingernail polish! For God's sake, you're spitting it all over my best sari!"

She slapped me.

I punched her in the stomach.

After that, I didn't call for her much, and if I did, she would say, "I am not your ayah," or "Call Vimla."

Auntie Vimla was Mamaji's third sister, but I didn't like calling her, because whenever she saw me she would start crying. "My poor blind lamb!" she would say. "God pity you!"

Auntie Pushpa and Auntie Vimla were only a little older than Sister Pom. Yet whenever we stayed in Mozang Road they used to boss us around and tease us constantly. They had nicknames for us: Sister Pom was Lal Mirch (red chili), because, they said, if any one of us was insulted by any one of them, Sister Pom, without waiting to find out the rights and wrongs, would burn; Sister Nimi was Parrol Shas (fat lord), because, they said, she had a lordly indifference; Sister Umi was Gol-guppi (a pungent savory), because, they said, she couldn't control her sharp tongue; Brother Om was Princey, because, they said, he was the Prince of Wales of our family; and I was Master Sahib, because, they said, I looked studious, even if I couldn't read. Usha, as yet, had not rated a nickname.

Daddyji had told us that making up such names was a pastime of frivolous society people. And, indeed, Babuji had a title from the British and was independently wealthy. Certainly, as my big sisters never tired of pointing out, Auntie Pushpa and Auntie Vimla conducted themselves as they imagined ladies of fashion did. They insisted that we call them "Auntie," because they thought that the English form of address was more elegant. (They also insisted that we call their brothers

"Uncle.") Auntie Pushpa even kept her fingernails long and wore lipstick and scent—things that no Mehta girl was permitted to do. It was said that Auntie Pushpa was more beautiful than any other girl in either the Mehra or the Mehta clan, and that she had expensive tastes in clothes, in scents, and in jewelry.

"We don't give a hoot for title, money, or fashion," Sister Umi, who had cast herself as our spokesman, would say to Auntie Pushpa. "Our Daddyji is a government officer. There is a respect that goes with government service which no amount of Babuji's money can buy for him."

"But Babuji has a title," Auntie Pushpa would say. "You can't get away from that. So there, Golguppi!"

"I'll call you Auntie because I respect Mamaji, but you are no auntie of mine," Sister Umi would say. "You don't respect me, I don't respect you."

"You're not fit to lick my shoes," Auntie Pushpa would say. "You Mehtas are all buffalo brains and paratha bodies." The aunties drank the lighter cow's milk; we drank the heavier buffalo's milk. They ate the lighter chapattis; we ate the heavier parathas (unleavened wheat bread). Daddyji, in the course of his work, had seen a lot of malnutrition and tuberculosis, and he was much concerned with our diet.

"I'd rather be a buffalo brain than a nervous cat," Sister Umi would say. The aunties were constantly going on about their delicate digestions and their headaches. We never complained of anything.

"You are not fit to live in this house among polite people," Auntie Pushpa would say. "You Mehtas are all alike—rowdies and toughies. Are your Balwant Chachaji and your Raj Kanwar Chachaji black sheep of the family or not? Tell me!" *Chacha* means paternal uncle. Balwant Chachaji, a mild-mannered man who had frittered away his time at college, had ended up as a sort of tailor in a parachute factory, and Raj Kanwar Chachaji, a hot-tempered, quarrelsome man, who had also wasted his time at college, had ended up as chief of a succession of police stations.

"We Mehtas are good at whatever we do," Sister Umi would say. "If we are rowdies and toughies, we are the best rowdies and toughies. If we are failures, we are the best failures. And, by the way, you should thank your stars that you have our buffalo brains and paratha bodies around to press Manji's legs, arms, and back."

Manji was Mataji's long-widowed mother (our great-grandmother), who mostly lived with Babuji and Mataji in Mozang Road, because her only son (our great-uncle), Shiv Das, who would otherwise have been her staff and support, had never amounted to much. She had no money of her own, and was constantly trying to make herself useful, sewing new quilts for the family or attending to the old quilts—unstitching them, removing the matted cotton, having it carded and combed, and then stitching it back into them. She also daily ground with millstones the oats for Babuji's porridge, to the exact texture he liked—he liked his porridge on the coarse side. She was very fat and was always having aches and pains. Sometimes her aches and pains would become so severe that she couldn't move. We would help her apply Hakimji's Green Ointment to her arms and legs, and would help bandage them by pulling at the gauze to make it tight. This gave her some relief. Then she would lie face down, and, following her directions, one of us would stand on her, leaning on the pole of a mosquito net so as to take some of our weight off her. In this way, we would carefully walk up and down her arms, her back, and her legs, staying on the balls of our feet. If, accidentally, we put all our weight on her or put a heel down, she would cry out.

The aunties considered themselves too ladylike to press Manji for long, but we could do it for an hour at a time. They also considered themselves too ladylike to go frequently with Manji to the temple inside the old, crowded, fetid city—something she did regularly. We Mehtas, except for Brother Om, enjoyed going with her, and whenever we went she would buy us little presents—balloons for me, glass bangles for my big sisters. Even if the balloons and bangles were of the cheapest variety, a dozen for an anna, the aunties would be jealous of us and find an excuse to scold us.

Sometimes our quarrels with the aunties would get so heated that we would forget how nice to us they could be—they were always bringing us presents and fluttering over us—and we would threaten to leave. We'd actually start walking toward the gate. Then the aunties would come running after us, because they feared Babuji and Daddyji.

"What's there to fear about Daddyji?" Sister Umi once asked Mamaji.

"You children have grown up on your father's shoulders, and you fear nothing," Mamaji said. "We drank our mother's milk. She has always been afraid of

Babuji, so we have all grown up with a fear of the man of the house."

My big sisters often wanted to go and tattle on the aunties to Babuji and teach them a lesson, but, as a concession to the aunties' fear of Babuji, they would tattle to Mataji instead. They soon learned that in Mataji's eyes, at least, Auntie Pushpa could do no wrong. "Pushpa is my special darling," Mataji would say. We didn't know what she meant by that until at last she explained to us, "A pandit has told me that as long as Pushpa flourishes the whole family will flourish."

One day, Auntie Pushpa came out of the bathroom and announced, "Look! I've cut off all my hair. Now I have bobbed hair, like the most fashionable English ladies."

My big sisters cried out in dismay.

"Our Daddyji says, 'Hair is a woman's crowning glory,' and look what you've done to yourself!" Sister Pom said.

"Our Mamaji has never even touched a scissors to her long hair, and still she won't go in front of men without covering her head," Sister Nimi said.

"Babuji will beat you with his walking stick," Sister Umi said.

I waited for Babuji to take his walking stick to Auntie Pushpa, but I never heard him so much as scold her.

Many years later, Daddyji explained to us that Auntie Pushpa had a special place not only in Mataji's heart but also in Babuji's. "By the time Pushpa was born, Babuji had lost seven of his children at birth or in childhood, and an eighth died before Pushpa was five weeks old," he said. "As a baby, Pushpa herself was so frail that he wasn't sure she would live. Five of the children who died were born to Mataji—she is Babuji's second wife—and as a result she became very superstitious."

"Like our Mamaji," Sister Umi said.

"Correct," Daddyji said.

As a child, I wasn't sure what "superstitious" meant, but I remember that one evening—it was the night before Uncle Dwarka, the elder of Mamaji's two younger brothers, was due to leave for a journey—Mataji called the gardener over. "Take tomorrow off," she told him.

We were all puzzled, because she never gave the gardener a day off like that.

The next morning, as Uncle Dwarka was leaving the house, she shouted to the sweeper, "Jamadar, come and sweep the garden! The gardener isn't here today."

I later found out that the gardener was a Brahman, and that Mataji believed that anyone who sees a Brahman's face early in the morning before a journey will be ill-fated in it. Mataji had contrived to have Uncle Dwarka see the sweeper—an Untouchable, and so the complete opposite of a Brahman—before setting out.

The night after Uncle Dwarka left, when we were all in our beds in the children's bedroom, Sister Umi said, "Remember what Mataji started saying after Vedi went away to school?"

I lay very still in my bed, feeling sure that if Sister Umi knew I was awake she wouldn't go on. My big sisters and the aunties always sent Brother Om and me out of the room when they were talking about anything interesting.

"Mataji would say, 'Girls, you have only one whole brother left now,' " Sister Umi resumed. "And how she spoiled Om in those days by constantly calling him Prince of Wales! And our aunties didn't help matters by calling him Princey all the time."

"Just imagine calling him Prince of Wales and then putting frocks on him!" Sister Nimi said, laughing. She laughed so hard that she had difficulty catching her breath, and I couldn't keep quiet anymore and burst out laughing.

Sister Pom was very angry. "Umi, you have no sense. Nimi, stop it. Vedi, go to sleep."

"How was I to know that the cunning So-and-So was listening?" Sister Umi asked. "I heard Om snoring away, so I assumed Vedi was asleep, too."

"I'll go to sleep if you tell me why they put frocks on Brother Om," I said. But Sister Pom had such control over Sisters Nimi and Umi that I couldn't get them to say. Years later, I finally learned the reason for the frocks: Mamaji had attributed my blindness to the vengeance of the evil eye for my being a healthy, handsome boy. To ward off the evil eye from Om, she would dress him up in frocks.

SISTER UMI ALWAYS said that Brother Om was the only one of us children who took after the Mehras in temperament. Except for Babuji, who didn't play favorites, everyone at 16 Mozang Road seemed to be partial to Brother Om. Mataji was always getting new clothes made for him, and the aunties were always bringing him special sweets.

I remember that once when Brother Om came back from Bishop Cotton School on a holiday Auntie Pushpa ran over to him and said, "Princey, what a sahib you look in your sola topi!"

As soon as I heard the phrase "sola topi," I wanted to know what it was. Brother Om showed me his sola topi, pointing out its various features. It had a thick, sloping brim to keep out the sun, an adjustable leather chin strap to hold it firmly in place in a strong wind, a leather rim to absorb sweat, and four nostril-like rubber tabs near the top for air. "Only Britishers could have designed such a perfect headgear for the rotten Indian sun," Brother Om said.

I struggled to push the chin strap up over the front of the brim to get it out of the way, and asked, "What is this delicate sound I hear from inside the sola topi?"

"It's the pith stuffed inside," Brother Om said. "That's what makes it so thick and yet so light." The hat was as solid as a helmet but almost as light as a silk turban.

I remember that Brother Om used to wear his sola topi even inside, in the cool of the house, chanting, "My name is Om Parkash Mehta. I am a sahib in sola topi. I go to Bishop Cotton School, in Simla. Simla is where the Viceroy goes for his summers. I am a sahib in sola topi."

One day, my big sisters, my big brother, and I were washing our hands and faces on the steps of the front

veranda after having our tiffin, as was our practice.
Brother Om leaned over to rinse his mouth and almost
dropped his sola topi. As he reached out to catch it, he
happened to splash some water on Babuji, who was
passing by in his long coat on the way to some formal
party.

Brother Om started howling, "Babuji beat me with
his walking stick!"

My big sisters had been busy washing and hadn't
seen what had happened, and there had been so much
noise of water splashing that I didn't know what had
happened, either. But none of us doubted that Brother
Om had been beaten. We would have run after Babuji
and protested, but he had already been driven away in
his car.

"How dare Babuji beat us, when our own father
has never beaten us?" Sister Pom said. "I won't stay at
16 Mozang Road for one more minute." It was surprising to hear Sister Pom say that, and turn into the real
red chili that the aunties claimed she was.

We all swore to each other that we would not spend
another night under the roof of a man who beat children with a walking stick, even if that man happened
to be our grandfather. But though we felt we had to
leave at once, we didn't have the slightest idea where
to go. Daddyji was away on a long tour and had taken
Mamaji and Usha with him. We couldn't go to Mehta
Gulli, behind 16 Mozang Road, where all our closest
Mehta relatives lived, because we were afraid Babuji
would find out that we were there and have us brought
back to 16 Mozang Road.

"Where do birds and animals live?" Sister Nimi

asked boldly. "After all, they have no home to go to."

"Nimi, you're a genius," Sister Umi said. "We can go to Lawrence Gardens and live like birds and animals."

We five brothers and sisters all caught hold of one another's hands and walked away from 16 Mozang Road, without stopping to take so much as a toothbrush. It was late in the afternoon, and there was hardly any-body on the road. Occasionally, one of us would say something or cry, but mostly we walked silently.

"I'm glad to be free of those aunties," Sister Umi said. "The Mehras are a superstitious society lot. I want to have nothing to do with them ever again. I'm not a Mehra. I'm a Mehta through and through. I disown all the Mehras—the whole lot of them."

"Shush," Sister Pom said. "Your loose tongue will bring us bad luck."

At Lawrence Gardens, we huddled on a hill, under a tree, never admitting to ourselves that we were cold and frightened. Brother Om would begin crying, I would join in, Sister Nimi would follow, and before we knew it we would all be sobbing. We would stop just as suddenly as we had started, only to start again.

I listened to the crickets and thought that I had never heard anything sound so forlorn. I dozed. I was startled by the sound of something darting through the grass. I was frightened by the noise of wings beating in the trees. I noticed that my knickers were getting moist with dew. I heard the nightingales' mournful song. Then I thought I heard in the distance, "Pom Memsahi-ib! Nimi Memsahi-ib! Umi Memsahi-ib! Om Sahi-ib! Vedi Sahi-ib!" The voice sounded now close, as if it were inside my head, now far off, as if it were carried away by the wind. I couldn't make out whose voice it was, or even whether it was a voice at all. Then I heard the unmistakable voice of Sher Singh calling, "Pom Mem-sahi-ib!"

"Sher Singh, we are here!"

"We are here, Sher Singh!"

"Sher Singh, here!"

We were all calling him at once.

"Come," he said, as if we were back at 16 Mozang Road and he were summoning us to the dining room. "Come. Babuji and Mataji are waiting for you."

I expected at least Sister Umi to demur, but she didn't. All of us got up hurriedly and started back.

"So they prefer the company of fickle birds and animals to the company of their loyal servant," Sher Singh muttered to himself, walking behind us at a discreet distance. "What an evening Sher Singh has passed!"

After we got back to 16 Mozang Road, we learned that everyone had become alarmed when it was discovered that we were missing. Babuji had dispatched servants in all directions—to Mehta Gulli, to Kalu's house, next door, to Mozang Chowk, the nearest intersection— to try to find us. For all he knew, we had been kidnapped; he said to us that it had never occurred to him that we might have left without telling anyone or that he could in any way have been the cause of our leaving. Indeed, he insisted that he had only shaken his walking stick at Brother Om. Sher Singh had gone hither and thither and made inquiries, and had then decided on his own that we must be in the only place no one had thought of looking—Lawrence Gardens. "I thought, It's just the kind of thing Doctor Sahib's children are likely to do," he said to us.

For several days, the aunties made such a fuss over us—kissing us, calling us all "heroes," asking us every last detail—that even Sister Umi felt for a time proud to own them for our close relatives. All the same, we started spending more and more time in Mehta Gulli.

❦

To GET TO Mehta Gulli, we merely had to walk to the back of 16 Mozang Road and climb over a five-foot brick wall. Here the houses of our Mehta relatives were built along a *gulli,* or narrow street, in a sort of square, and had common walls. In Mehta Gulli, we all had Mehta cousins more or less our own ages. The cousins we spent most of our time with were the children of Daulat Ram Chachaji—Daddyji's next younger brother—who had received the same medical training as Daddyji, and who also worked in the Public Health Department. Daulat Ram Chachaji had five children. The two oldest were his daughters, Sheila and Leila, who were about Sister Pom's and Sister Nimi's ages and had been given names with the same ending as the names of my big sisters. (Pom, Nimi, and Umi were nicknames for Promila, Nirmila, and Urmila.) Cousins Sheila and Leila and my big sisters all went to the Sacred Heart Convent and played on the same school volleyball team. Cousin Yog, the oldest of Daulat Ram Chachaji's three sons, was three years older than Brother Om, and was the first Mehta boy in our generation. Whenever the boy cousins—or "cousin-brothers," as they are called—played a game, he was the leader. He chose the game, set the rules, and was the referee in any dispute. His brother Surinder was a year older than I was, and the youngest brother, Ravi, was a year older than Usha.

In Mehta Gulli, my big sisters and Cousins Sheila and Leila would sit on the veranda of Daulat Ram Chachaji's house, knitting and sewing and gossiping. One bit of gossip I remember overhearing was about an Irish nun at Sacred Heart who liked toffee. The girls were always giving her toffee, and the Mother Superior was always catching her chewing it and punishing her by making her say Hail Marys. The first time the nun was caught, she had to say five Hail Marys; the next time, ten. The more times she was caught, the more Hail Marys she had to say.

The cousin-brothers would play in the *gulli*. Sometimes, when they were playing a rough game, like tag, Cousin Yog would shunt Usha, Ravi, and me aside, but other times, when they were playing a slow game, like marbles, Cousin Yog would let us stand around and watch or listen.

I liked going to Mehta Gulli. Not so Brother Om. He liked to play with "the boarding-school sort," he said, and none of our cousins in Mehta Gulli went to boarding school. He also liked to play on grass, and Mehta Gulli had no grass—it was just cobblestones, with dirt on either side.

I remember one morning when we all went to Mehta Gulli. As usual, I stood on Sister Pom's shoulders, and Sister Nimi, who was the tallest and the first one over the wall, got me down on the other side. I could immediately tell that we had left the sedate Mehra world behind and arrived in the tumultuous Mehta world. There were the boisterous sounds of my older cousin-brothers playing a familiar game in the *gulli*—hitting a wooden peg around with a stick. The *gulli* was alive with the clack of the wooden stick repeatedly hitting the peg, the clatter of the peg bouncing off the cobblestones, and the patter of tennis shoes as a cousin-brother raced after the peg.

"Om, join us!" Cousin Yog called over, hitting the peg. "But first take off that silly topi!"

"A sola topi may be fine in your sissy Mozang Road, but now you're in Mehta Gulli!" Cousin Rajinder called over to us. He was Raj Kanwar Chachaji's oldest son and was our rowdiest cousin-brother.

"I don't go out in the sun without my sola topi," Brother Om said, "and I don't play street games with *mahashas, mhajas,* and *gamas." Mahashas, mhajas,* and *gamas* were common names for the lower orders—milkmen and the like—and they were our aunties' nicknames for our rowdy Mehta cousin-brothers.

"What did you say?" Cousin Surinder called back.

"I said I play cricket and hockey with the boarding-school sort on the grass."

"Who did you call *mhajas* and *gamas?"* Cousin Rajinder cried, running up to Brother Om. All the cousin-brothers surrounded Brother Om.

"Trying to give yourself airs, with your boarding-school topi and your grandfather's grass!" Cousin Yog said.

I heard the sola topi hit the street.

"Look! You've got mud on my sola topi!" Brother Om cried. "You're all dirty street boys!"

Cousins Yog, Surinder, and Rajinder started shouting threats like "We would beat the sola topi out of you if girls weren't standing here!"

Daulat Ram Chachaji came out of his house. "Om, you go to sahib school and there you learn to look down on your own Mehta brothers," he said. "And, Yog, you forget that, sahib or not, he's still your Mehta brother. Now let me see all you brothers play like brothers."

With Daulat Ram Chachaji standing there, everyone quickly made peace. Brother Om agreed to play with the cousin-brothers if they didn't make fun of his sola topi, and the cousin-brothers agreed to play with him as long as he never called them names again.

ONE EVENING at 16 Mozang Road, Mamaji called us all to her and said, "Let's go and have some fun in Mehta Gulli."

"Mamaji having fun in Mehta Gulli!" we cried. "That's a change. What's the big reason?"

Unlike my big sisters and me, Mamaji never particularly liked going to Mehta Gulli. Like Brother Om, she preferred 16 Mozang Road—even though, as the wife of the oldest Mehta brother, she was greatly respected by our *chachas* and *chachis*. (*Chachi* means "paternal uncle's wife.") "Mehta Gulli is full of Mehta demons, and each of them is bolder than the next," she would say. "O my mother, O God, save me from those Mehta in-laws!"

With a mysterious air, she now said, "No reason." Then she added, "I think there are new persons there."

"Who?" we cried.

"New persons," she said.

"I don't like the old persons there," Brother Om said. "What do I care about new persons?"

Brother Om ran away. The rest of us rushed to the back wall with Mamaji, and we all climbed over it in no time.

"Which house?" we asked.

"Romesh Chachaji's house," Mamaji said. Romesh Chachaji was Daddyji's fourth brother.

We ran through Mehta Gulli to Romesh Chachaji's house, at the far end—I was holding on to Sister Pom's hand—and raced up the stairs to the upper story. Even before we had finished climbing the stairs, I heard what I can only describe as "tick-tock" cries. There was first a soft "tick" cry, which was promptly answered by a loud "tock" cry, and before the loud cry had subsided, the soft cry had started up again. The alternating cries were so rhythmic that I could have tapped my foot to them.

"Those are the new persons," Mamaji said, puffing and wheezing behind us on the stairs. "Romesh's wife has given birth to two babies."

"Two babies at once from Savitri Chachiji!" Sister Umi cried. "Savitri Chachiji must be a magician!"

We had never heard of two babies arriving at once. We had no idea that such a thing was possible in the whole world.

Upstairs, on Romesh Chachaji's terrace, Sister Nimi

took my hand and put it on what seemed like a flailing bundle in Savitri Chachiji's arms. It had four legs, four arms, and two heads, like a toy god.

"It's one person!" I cried, pulling my hand back.

Mamaji laughed. "Innocent, it's not one person but two!"

Savitri Chachiji sat me down on a cot and put in my lap first one baby and then the other. "This is your Cousin-Brother Vijay," she said, cooing, "and this is your Cousin-Sister Usha—now there will be two Usha Mehtas."

I couldn't stop laughing, thinking of calling such small babies cousin-brother and cousin-sister and of their one day calling me cousin-brother.

Afterward, when we were out in the *gulli,* Sister Umi said, "There is nothing to equal a love marriage— I think I would like one."

Romesh Chachaji and Savitri Chachiji had made a love marriage, like film stars. It was said that he had arrived in Mehta Gulli with her without any warning and shocked all our *chachas* and *chachis,* cousin-brothers and cousin-sisters by announcing, "This is my love-marriage bride." After that, it seemed there was hardly a day when there wasn't a new, shocking discovery about her. She was a Marathi girl from Bombay and didn't speak a word of Punjabi; she was an Indian Christian and had no caste; she was a nurse and had met Romesh Chachaji while nursing him in the hospital. We children got really excited when we discovered that she could speak English—something that none of our mothers could do.

"Savitri Chachiji will give us free lessons in English," Cousin Sheila said, parading around Mehta Gulli.

I remember that Sister Umi said, "Cousin Sheila is a little weak in English, and the idea that she might get a jump on her classmates by a little free home tuition really thrills her."

"Be fair," Sister Nimi said. "We are all thrilled. After all, the only ladies we know who are Christians and work and speak English are the Sacred Heart nuns, and here in Mehta Gulli is a lady who is all those things and, on top of it, she is our *chachi.*"

"Well, all I can say is that our *chachi* is very progressive," Sister Umi said. "While the nuns are praying in their chapel, she goes out and catches our gullible *chacha* in a love marriage."

Everyone in Mehta Gulli remarked on how exceptionally attentive Romesh Chachaji was to Savitri Chachiji. One afternoon, Balwant Chachaji, who was standing in the doorway of his house, looked up and saw Romesh Chachaji standing on the terrace of his house and doing something a man had not been seen doing, as Balwant Chachaji later put it, "at least since Alexander the Great Sahib came to Lahore." Romesh Chachaji was taking down a petticoat from the clothesline. As Balwant Chachaji gawked, unseen, Romesh Chachaji shook the petticoat to make sure it was dry and then hooked a drawstring to a toothbrush and tenderly pushed it through the waist of the petticoat until it emerged on the other side. The whole action probably did not take more than a couple of minutes, but it was long enough for Balwant Chachaji to serenade Romesh

Chachaji with a song, which he said came to him just out of the sky:

I have mastered English;
I have visited the fashionable Anarkali;
My lord and master puts a drawstring in my petticoat—
Only then do I wear my petticoat.
My lord and master helps me hold up my petticoat;
He is my fashionable petticoat from Anarkali.

As Balwant Chachaji sang, all the Mehta women within reach of his serenading voice came to their windows or out onto their terraces and watched as Romesh Chachaji retreated sheepishly into his house with the petticoat. In this way, he gained a reputation as the only henpecked husband in Mehta Gulli; and in time, wherever the name Mehta was known in Lahore—whether in Mehta Gulli or the bazaar of Anarkali—the song "I have mastered English" was known and crooned.

ONE DAY, SHER SINGH returned from leave in his village in the Kangara District, in the hills, with a baby myna for me. "I have brought you a friend," he said. "It's a baby myna. It's one of the only birds in the world that can talk. It's just the right age to learn to talk."

I was excited. I went with Sher Singh to the Mozang Chowk and bought a wire cage with a door, a metal floor, and a little swing. The cage had a hook at the top, and I hung it in my room. (We were temporarily living in our own house, at 11 Temple Road.) I got a couple of brass bowls—one for water, the other for grain—and filled them up and put them in the cage. I got a brush for cleaning out the cage. I named the myna Sweetie. The name came to me just out of the sky.

"How do you catch a baby myna?" I asked Sher Singh.

"It's difficult, Vedi Sahib. There are very few of them around, and you have to know where a baby myna is resting with her mother. You have to slip up on them in the middle of the night, when they are sleeping in their nest, and throw a cover over them and hope that you catch the baby, because only a baby myna can learn to talk. Sometimes the mother myna will nip at your finger, and there are people in my village who are constantly getting their fingers nipped at because they have been trying to catch a baby myna."

At first, Sweetie was so small that she could scarcely fly even a few inches. I would sit her on my shoulder and walk around the room. She would dig her nervous, trembling claws through my shirt and into my shoulder as she tried to keep her balance, fluttering around my ear and sending off little ripples of air. But Sweetie grew fast, and soon she was flying around my room. Before I opened her cage to fill up the bowls or clean the floor, I would have to shut the door. She would often nip at my finger and escape from the cage. She would go and perch on the mantelpiece. When I ran to the mantelpiece to catch her, she would fly up to the curtain rod. When I climbed up onto the windowsill and shook the curtain, she would fly back to the mantel- piece. Sometimes she would be so silent that I would wonder if she was still in the room. Other times, I would hear her flying all around the room—now she would be by the window, now by the overhead light, her wings beating against the pane and the lampshade. I would make kissing sounds, as I had heard Sher Singh make them. I would call to her—"Sweetie! Sweetie!" I would whistle affectionately. I would run frenetically from one end of the room to the other. I would scream with rage. But she wouldn't come to me. I would somehow have to summon Sher Singh through the closed door, and then give him a cue to come in when I thought she wasn't near the door, and he would have to prance around the room and somehow catch her with his duster.

"She's a real hill girl, all right, flying around like that," he would say.

When we had finally got her back in the cage, I would scold her roundly, but it didn't seem to do much good.

"Vedi Sahib, you'll lose her, like your eyes, if you don't keep her always in the cage," Sher Singh said.

"But then how can I feed her? How can I clean out her cage?"

"I will do all that, Vedi Sahib. And, because I can see, I can watch her."

"But I like looking after her," I said.

"You'll lose her, Vedi Sahib," he said. "And mind your finger. She's getting big."

I devised a way of filling her bowls and cleaning some of the cage's floor by surreptitiously sticking my fingers between the wires. But now and again I would want to feel her on her swing or take her out and hold her, and then she would nip at my finger and sometimes draw blood. She would escape and give me a real run around the room.

Every time I passed Sweetie's cage, I would say "Hello, Sweetie," and wait for her to talk. But she would only flutter in the cage or, at most, make her swing squeak.

"Are you sure Sweetie can talk?" I asked Sher Singh.

"All baby mynas from Kangara can learn to talk," he said.

"Are you sure she is from Kangara?"

"Only mynas from Kangara have a black patch on the throat. You can feel it, and you can ask anyone—it's as black as coal."

I took Sweetie out of her cage. I held her tight in one hand and tried to feel the patch on her throat with the other. She screamed and tried to bite my finger, but I finally found the patch. It was a little soft, downy raised circle that throbbed with her pulse.

"What do mynas sound like when they talk?" I later asked Sher Singh.

"They have the voice of the Kangara, of a Kangara hill girl."

"What is that?"

"The Punjab hills, the leaves in the wind, the waterfall on a mountainside—you know, Vedi Sahib, it's the sound of a peacock spreading its wings in Kangara at dawn."

One day, I passed her cage and said, "Hello. Sweetie."

"Hello, Sweetie," she answered.

I jumped. I don't know how I had expected her voice to sound, but it was thin, sharp, and defiant—at once whiny and abrasive—like three treble notes on the harmonium played very fast. Her words assaulted my ears—"Sweetie" was something that film stars called each other on the screen, and sounded very naughty.

I had scarcely taken in the fact that Sweetie could really speak when she repeated "Hello, Sweetie." She kept on repeating it, hour after hour. "Hello, Sweetie" would suddenly explode into the air like a firecracker.

Try as I would, I couldn't teach her to say anything else. All the same, there was something thrilling and comforting in having my own film star in the cage, and I got so used to her enticing outbursts that I missed them when she kept quiet or was dozing.

Every evening, at the time when my big sisters and my big brother went to play hockey or some other game with their school friends, it was Sher Singh's duty to take me for a walk to Lawrence Gardens. There I would ride the merry-go-round—a big, creaky thing with wooden seats and a metal railing—while Sher Singh ran alongside. It would revolve and lurch, tipping this way and that way, filling me with terror and excitement. On the ground, I would throw off my shoes and run up and down the hillocks. They were covered with damp, soft grass and occasional patches of dead grass. The grass would caress, tickle, and prick my feet. All around, there were the light, cheerful sounds of sighted children running and playing and of birds flying and perching and calling. In the distance, there was the solitary, mournful song of a nightingale.

I felt sorry that Sweetie, shut up in the house,

couldn't enjoy the company of other birds, and one evening I insisted that we take her along in her cage and let her enjoy the fresh air and the life of Lawrence Gardens, even if it was only through the wires of her cage.

"But don't let her out of the cage," Sher Singh said. "She is a spirit from the hills. She will fly back to Kangara."

"Fly all the way to Kangara! She would die without food or water. Besides, she is my friend. She wouldn't leave me."

"Vedi Sahib, you know how loyal Kangara servants are?"

"No one could be more loyal than you, Sher Singh."

"Well, Kangara mynas are as disloyal as Kangara servants are loyal. You can love a beloved myna all you want to, give her all the grain to eat you want to, give her all the water to drink you want to, and at the first opportunity she will nip at your finger and fly away. But you can kick a servant from Kangara and he will still give you first-class service."

"Why is that?"

"Because servants from Kangara, like mynas, have breathed the Himalayan air and are free spirits. A Kangara servant is a servant by choice—but no myna is in a cage by choice."

I couldn't follow exactly what Sher Singh was saying, but I laughed. Anyway, I insisted that we take Sweetie with us.

At Lawrence Gardens, I had no intention of taking Sweetie out of her cage, but when she heard the other birds she set up such a racket that children and servants who usually took little notice of me wandered toward us to find out what I was doing to the poor myna. They said all kinds of things:

"She is lonely."

"He's keeping her a prisoner."

"Tch, tch! He can't play with other children, so he won't let his myna play with other birds."

"She'll fly away to Kangara!" I cried.

People laughed, hooted, and jeered. "She's so small she probably can't even fly up to that tree."

"Why are you pointing? He doesn't know how high that tree is."

I suddenly got an idea. I had with me a ball of strong, fortified string that Brother Om used for flying kites. I took Sweetie out of the cage and, while I held her screaming and biting in my hands, I had Sher Singh tie up her legs with the string. Then I caught hold of the ball and let her go, and the people about us clapped and cheered. I started giving her string, and she flew high up and pulled and tugged. I gave her more string and let her lead me where she would around the grass. I thought it was a wonderful game. Before I knew what had happened, her weight at the end of the string was gone, and the limp string had fluttered down on me.

"She's bitten through the string! Look, she's bitten through the string!" everyone shouted, running away.

"Sher Singh, catch her! Catch her!" I cried. "Bring Sweetie back!"

"I think I see her!" he called, running off.

A few minutes later, Sher Singh came back. "She's nowhere to be found, Vedi Sahib. She's gone, Sahib—

gone straight back to Kangara. You will now have to get along without Sweetie."

Sher Singh and I looked for her all over Lawrence Gardens, calling "Sweetie! Sweetie!" until it was dark and everyone had left. Then Sher Singh and I walked home with the empty cage.

ONCE WHEN DADDYJI was posted in Ambala, he took a cottage for us in nearby Simla for the summer. I remember that at the time my big sisters were worried about being short and ending up like our Mehra relatives, who were all short. (Except for Om, none of us started growing tall until we were in our early teens.) Hakimji had told us that the only remedy for shortness he knew of in the ancient books was to go on the swings and swing as high as one could. "That will stretch your neck and your legs and make you shoot up like a mushroom," he had said.

Our cottage was halfway up Jakko Hill, and there was a ladies' park below us. Every day, my big sisters would go and spend the afternoon there swinging, but they wouldn't take me. I complained to Mamaji.

"You know they are your father's daughters," she said. "They have the Mehta demon in them. I am only a Mehra. I can't get them to listen."

I waited until Daddyji, who was away on tour, came back, and then I complained to him.

"You must take Vedi along," he told my big sisters. "He will enjoy going on a swing."

"But, Daddyji, it's the ladies' park, and there is a

watchman!" Sister Umi cried. "There are no boys there over five, and Vedi is older than that."

"Never mind about that," Daddyji said. "Just take him."

The next day, when my big sisters were walking to the ladies' park, I skipped along at Sister Pom's side, thinking about being on a swing every day and becoming taller than Abdul, who couldn't afford to have Hakimji for a doctor and so couldn't know about the benefit of going on the swings every day.

At the ladies' park, the watchman wouldn't let me in.

"But he can't see," Sister Nimi said, "so the ladies won't mind him."

"Can't see! Why didn't you say so before, Memsahib?" The watchman bent over me, clicked his tongue, and sighed. "As Ram is my witness, I couldn't have told by looking at him. If Sahib were twenty or thirty years old, the ladies couldn't mind him. Take him in, Memsahibs. Let God give him courage."

After that, the watchman would cluck over me every day and wonder aloud how it was that he had ever imagined I could be a threat to any lady's modesty. Every day, I would go on the swings with one or another of my big sisters and pray to Jesus, Mary, and Joseph to make me taller than Abdul.

IN SIMLA ONCE, Sister Pom was trying to snatch a sewing needle from Sher Singh, who wouldn't give it to her. "You're too small to use a needle," he said.

I wondered why Sher Singh was being so silly about the needle; at school, I sewed my own buttons on.

"Pom Memsahib, you can use the needle when you can get it down by yourself," he said, doing something over his head, and he went out of the room.

"Look, he's hung it on the beam," Sister Umi said.

Sister Pom climbed up on to the mantelpiece. "Oh, I've dropped it," she said, and she jumped down. She screamed, "My heel! The needle has gone in!"

"Oh, it's broken," Sister Umi said, picking up something from the carpet.

We all burst out crying. Daddyji happened to come in from outside, and he hurried Sister Pom in a rickshaw to the clinic. There the doctors operated on her heel, and for many weeks afterward she couldn't walk.

"What would have happened to her if they hadn't been able to get the needle out?" I asked Daddyji.

"It could have travelled with her blood to some other part of her body, and that could have been very dangerous."

"Why hasn't Sher Singh been punished?"

"He didn't know any better, and accidents can happen at any time."

For some time, I went around feeling angry at Sher Singh. Then I forgot all about him, because I became interested in how Sister Pom had to learn to walk all over again. Because she was afraid to put her weight on her injured foot, she had trouble walking straight. One day, Daddyji took her to a two-lane macadamized road nearby, and I went along. He had her practice walking straight on the white line that separated the two lanes; there was no traffic, because only three cars—those of the top British officials—were permitted in Simla. He asked her to put one foot in front of the other on the white line while he stood some distance ahead of her and clapped encouragingly. I wanted to know whether Sister Pom was walking straight, so she let me crawl alongside her with my hands on her feet as she walked. I remembered in a rush the rope. After the meningitis, my big sisters would daily help me practice walking on the lawn of 16 Mozang Road with the rope. Sister Nimi and Sister Umi would stand holding it stretched between them, and I would walk with my hand on it. Sister Pom would crawl at my side with her hands on my feet (much as Mr. Ras Mohun did later on). I had come to think that, in my family, sickness and forgetting how to walk were peculiar to me, but here was Sister Pom having the same trouble.

"Vedi, am I walking correctly?" she asked from above my head.

"You're doing very well," I called up to her.

I WAS BACK AT SCHOOL for what proved to be the last time. (The year was 1943.) There was a new teacher, who lived outside the school and came only part time, not to teach subjects but to introduce us to a special new game. "It's a very old game," he said. "It's a game that came before your school, before Braille was thought of, before the arithmetic slate was made, before there ever was a blind person—before a man was born. The gods used to play it. In fact, that's how the game of man began.

"The big god and his courtesan played, sitting next to each other with the board between them, just as you and I are sitting next to each other on this bed, except that they sat on his throne. He was all eyes. She was naked except for a full-sleeved blouse, which she wore so that she could hide her pet mouse in her sleeve. He had never lost a game, but now she had the mouse at the ready.

" 'You have the light pieces,' she said. 'You have the first move.'

"He played his best game, but every time he looked at the board he saw he was losing. He couldn't understand it. Every time she put her hand out toward her dark pieces to make a move, the mouse would slip out of her sleeve, rearrange the board under the cover of her hands so slightly that it was hardly noticeable, and jump back into her sleeve. He lost.

" 'What will you have?' he said, in a voice of thunder. 'Ask for anything.'

" 'A man to take to bed with me,' she said.

"The mouse peeked out of her sleeve. He caught sight of it and made it into a man for her.

"That's how old the game is. Hold out your hands."

I put my hands out. They had been quivering to touch the game to find out what it was.

"Palms up." The new teacher dropped into my hands a number of smooth wooden pieces, many of them of different shapes. There was a hollowed-out circle with a decorated edge; an oblong with a rounded head and two points sticking up from the back like ears; a round bulb with a little slit near the top; a crowned head; a flat-topped round plane. There were many small pieces like tapering candlesticks. The shapes of the pieces suggested whole games in themselves. I counted the pieces: there were thirty-two. Half had little points sticking out from the top; the other half were smooth. All the pieces, big and small, with points and without points, had little pegs at the bottom.

The game was played on a board, a checked Bakelite surface with recessed squares, called white, and raised squares, called black, each with a hole in it for the pegs on the pieces. We lined up the pieces on the board for the game—the ones with points (white) on one side, the ones without points (black) on the other. They made the most exquisite symmetrical design under my hands. If on one side the crowned head stood on a recessed square, on the opposite side its likeness, facing it, stood on a raised square, and all the pieces on each side alternated in their height, depending on whether they were standing on recessed squares or raised squares. Between the two sides was a battlefield of alternating high ground and low ground.

"The pieces under your hand are foot soldiers and castles and horses, camels and queens and kings," the teacher was saying. "Every man or animal has his own walk and step. The foot soldier can go only forward and can go only one step at a time and only when the path is clear. The horse can go backward or forward, whether the path is clear or not, but it must always jump two steps, in whichever direction, and then one step left or right. The camels can go only diagonally. This white camel"—he showed me the camel on my right—"can walk only on the raised squares of the board. And this camel"—he showed me the camel on my left—"only on the recessed squares. Provided their paths are clear, they can race diagonally from one end of the board to the other. The castles can also race from one end of the board to the other, and from side to side, but they can't go diagonally—only in a straight line. So they are free to move from a raised square to a recessed square, as the camels are not. A queen can walk or she can race either like a camel or like a castle, but she is forbidden to jump like a horse.

"The point of the game is a struggle with the opponent's forces. Queens and castles, horses and camels can eat anything that is in the way of their walk or step, but a foot soldier cannot eat things in the way of his walk or step; he can eat only things diagonally in front of him. The poor king can go only one step at a time, but then everyone else on his side has only one function in the game—to protect the king. The king can eat anyone in the way of his walk or step, but everyone is forbidden to eat the king. He can only be surrounded and defeated."

"Who's forbidden them?" I asked. My head was full of questions.

"The gods," the teacher said.

After this first lesson from Mr. Chesswallah—for that is who the new teacher was, and the game was the Indian version of chess—I became an avid player. I would spend hours sitting with Deoji on his bed and playing chess.

Deoji always took a long time to make his move, and his hands studied the pieces, going over them again and again, the wooden pieces shaking and rattling in their Bakelite holes like trees in a storm. I would sit wondering which pieces Deoji's hands were concentrating on. Did he know, for instance, that my horse was about to eat his foot soldier? If he did know it, why was he taking so long to make his move? Surely his best move was to bring his threatened foot soldier one square up and threaten my horse. Perhaps he was trying to lull me by letting my horse eat his foot soldier, so that he could later trap my queen. I was eager to get my hands on the board, because I couldn't remember exactly where all his pieces were in relation to my queen. But the rules of the game forbade me to touch the board during his move.

"Hurry up, Deoji!" I called out.

"I know, I know," he said. "But this boy is slow. I don't know why you moved your horse there."

I wanted to tell him about his threatened foot soldier, because I realized that, in his good-hearted way, he had not understood that my horse was about to eat it. But the rules of the game forbade my putting him on notice, just as they forbade him to take back a move after he had made it.

"This boy needs more time to think," he said.

While I waited, I imagined that I was playing an altogether different kind of chess game, and that my opponent was the terrible Sighted Master. In that game, the boys' dormitory was the board, each bed being a raised square and the aisle between two beds a recessed square. I had the superior white. Ramesh was one of my foot soldiers, Jaisingh my castle, Abdul my horse, Bhaskar my camel, Paran my queen, and I was the king, commanding them all. I ordered Abdul to gallop three steps forward and one step to the right side and eat the Sighted Master's queen, but Abdul wouldn't obey. "I am only a horse—I can go only two steps forward at a time," he said. "Those are the rules of the game."

"Deoji, who made the rules of the game?" I now asked.

"That's like asking who made the game." The board rattled under the storm of his hands. "Why are you asking?"

"Just to know. Why can't we make our own rules?"

"But then it wouldn't be the game."

"Does the whole world play by these rules?"

"I think so. But Mr. Chesswallah did tell me that an Englishman moves foot soldiers two steps in the beginning of the game. That may be so, but we are not Englishmen. We are only the Indian blind sort, playing chess in the boys' dormitory."

In my imagined game, I ordered Ramesh, Jaisingh, Abdul, and Bhaskar to charge the Sighted Master, but they protested: "The rules of the game."

"I am moving my castle here," Deoji said.

I reached out and studied the board. My queen was safe.

"My horse is going to eat your foot soldier."

"No, that is not so."

I took his hand, showed him my horse, and pointed out the path to his foot soldier.

"What a pity!" he said. "That foot soldier was a special favorite of mine. I was sure he was going to become a second queen for me. Now I've lost the game."

"You've only lost one foot soldier."

"No, the game is up. Let's start again."

❦

ONE MORNING WHEN we had all gathered in front of Mr. Ras Mohun's office to tell him about our dreams, he came out and said, "The war is coming to Bombay in a big way. Dadar may be bombed, and the school may have to be moved a hundred or so miles away, to the town of Ahmadnagar. From now on, you need not come to me with your dreams."

"What, no more sweets?" we all found ourselves saying, and then we felt frightened at what we had said, and expected Mr. Ras Mohun to threaten us with his ruler.

"I told you," he said irritably, perhaps not noticing how ashamed we felt. "The war is coming in a big way. Dadar may be bombed. The school may have to be moved."

Mr. Ras Mohun told me to come with him. I kept up as best I could with the click-click of his shoes, and followed him out of the general classroom, up the boys' staircase, into the sitting-and-dining room. He closed the door and asked me to sit down.

"I've had my breakfast," I said.

"We've all had our breakfast," he said, "but I want to inform you of something."

I sat down at my separate table and scratched my knees under it.

"I wrote to your father that he should send for you, because you would be safer in the Punjab than here in Bombay, and he agrees."

"I'm not going," I said. "I want to stay with Deoji, Abdul, and Paran."

"You know that the school only goes up through the fourth standard, and you have finished the fourth standard. You have absorbed all that our school has to offer. Since no immediate provision can be made for your studies in the West, because of the war, it's best that you go home."

"But Abdul is staying here."

"Abdul is going to make caning chairs his career, so he can stay at the school and always cane chairs. Besides, he has no family. What you need most now is the experience of family life. That will be most beneficial to you if, after the war, provision can be made for you to live and study in the West."

"When will the war be over?"

"Who knows? It may go on for years."

I thought about leaving the school for good after the fourth standard. Mamaji had left school after the fourth standard, and everyone at home said she was uneducated. "But Deoji has finished the fourth standard, and he stays here and studies at the sighted school," I said. "I can stay here and go with him to the American Marathi Mission High School."

"Why with Deoji?" he asked. "I had planned for you to study with Heea at the Scottish Orphanage. It's nearby and it's one of the best sighted schools. I had mentioned you to its principal, a Scottish gentleman and a good friend, and told him that you were quick to learn and curious about everything. He said that he would be happy to experiment with you."

The back of my neck began to itch, but I didn't want to risk bringing my hand out from under the table to scratch, in case Mr. Ras Mohun chastised me, so I half shook and half nodded my head and hoped the itching would go away.

"But all that was before the threat of the war coming to Bombay in a big way and our plans to move the school to Ahmadnagar if Dadar is bombed. As I started to tell you, your father has written to me now, asking Auntie, Heea, and me to take you back to the Punjab and have a holiday with you and your family. Auntie and I are delighted at the prospect of meeting your family and seeing the Punjab and perhaps going up to Kashmir. We've never been to that part of the country. I have all but finished my dreams chapter, and next week is a very good time for us all to leave."

I thought of Mr. and Mrs. Ras Mohun and Heea sitting at the table with Daddyji and Mamaji and my big sisters and my big brother and Usha. It was like having Daddyji, Mamaji, and Sister Umi come and live in the boys' dormitory. I started praying feverishly to Jesus, Mary, and Joseph for Hitler to come right then and bomb the school.

"You won't like it, Uncle," I said.

"What won't I like?"

"The Punjab. Sister Umi has a bomb."

"I've told you that my dreams chapter is finished. You don't need to trouble to remember any more dreams. It's up to you when you want to tell your friends that you won't be coming back to the school. You can go now."

❧

OF MR. AND MRS. RAS MOHUN's and Heea's tour of
the Punjab as Daddyji's guests I remember little. I recall
that I had to live with them wherever they lived and go
with them wherever they went—to Lahore, to Rawalpindi, to Murree Hills—for the month or so that they
were with us. I recall that I started going around saying,
"My name is Vedi Mehta Ras Mohun." I recall that
everyone exclaimed in private over how small and dark
Mr. and Mrs. Ras Mohun were and how fair, in com-
parison, Heea was, and over what a funny little voice
Mr. Ras Mohun had. I recall that Sister Umi said Mr.
Ras Mohun put so much oil on his hair that it made his
face all shiny. I recall that Mr. and Mrs. Ras Mohun exclaimed to everyone over the size of Daddyji's car, the
size of our house, the size of 16 Mozang Road, the size
of Mehta Gulli, the size of our families, the size of Daddyji's clubs, the size of the clubs' cricket grounds. They
exclaimed over how many times meat was produced at
the table, how fair-skinned everyone was, how healthy
everyone looked, how well my big sisters and big
brother spoke English.

One day, Mr. and Mrs. Ras Mohun decided to go
on a little holiday of their own to Kashmir, "the Swit-
zerland of India," which was a couple of days' journey
by car up a mountainous road from Murree. Just before
they went, I had a dream that I told to everyone at the
breakfast table.

"I went out with Auntie to buy my clothes, shoes,
and other things," I said. "I was going to England.
Uncle took me there. We travelled by boat. I saw the
seas, the oceans, the deserts. We reached London. I

stayed there for three years. I came back again with Uncle."

"That's a clever dream," Mr. Ras Mohun said. "I will include it in my book"—and he did.

I recall that when they drove away—Daddyji had lent them his car and arranged for a driver for them—I felt very sad. I wouldn't let go of Mrs. Ras Mohun's hand, and my tears wouldn't stop coming. "I don't want to be left behind!" I cried.

EPILOGUE

I ATTENDED DADAR SCHOOL FOR THE BLIND FROM the time I was a month shy of five until a month or so after my ninth birthday—from February, 1939, to May, 1943. For many years thereafter, I scarcely thought about the school. But when I was in my forties—on the other side of life's slope, as it were—and was earning my livelihood as a writer, I found myself thinking continually about the school and about my classmates, and wondering how life had treated them. Then I went to Bombay, a city in which I had spent little time since leaving the school, and listened to Marathi being spoken all around me, but I could understand only two words—*ikade* ("here") and *tikade* ("there"). Marathi, which had once been almost my first language, was totally lost to me, like the pain of a healed wound, and no amount of exposure to the sounds of the language could bring it back.

I went to the school. Dadar and the soot were still there. The school building was still there, exactly as I remembered it, between the two huge mills, but no one I knew was around anymore. It now functioned both as a school and as a full-fledged industrial workshop for the blind. (Weaving and broommaking had been added to the caning of chairs for the livelihood of the orphans.) The boys' dormitory was gone with the boys and men of my childhood; instead, the school and the entire building now housed only girls and women, with thin, shrinking, demented voices—it was as if the new residents were not only blind but also retarded. This made me wonder whether the school of my childhood had had the same atmosphere. The thought was depressing—the more so because I knew there was no way I could dispose of the question to my satisfaction, since the answer was a matter not of memory but of judgment and experience, which, as a boy, I could not have had. Nevertheless, my interest in meeting someone from my school past was only further aroused when, through inquiries at the school and at welfare societies for the blind, I discovered that Abdul had died of consumption when he was twenty-four, that Paran had also died of consumption, when she was fifteen or sixteen, and that Bhaskar, too, had died of consumption at an early age— no one seemed to know exactly when. What had they— and all the others—done after leaving the school, I wanted to know. It seemed that the most accomplished of them had ended up being masseurs or physiotherapists. *The sense of touch—fingers that read, fingers that explore, fingers that heal like the Green Ointment of Hakimji.* Deoji, however, was teaching at a school for the blind somewhere in central India. (In due course, I looked him up and we spent a couple of days together. He confirmed this fact and that fact, but what he really succeeded in confirming was the divide between us— both before, during, and after our first meeting, when I was a child, and before, during, and after our last meeting, when I was a man.) Oh, yes, but Rajas was in the city, I was told at the school. Didn't I remember her? She had been nine when I arrived at the school. She had done the best of all. She had married Mr. Hansoti, who was a successor of Mr. Ras Mohun. But he had since died. She lived in a tenement, where I was free to go and meet her.

The entrance to the tenement is surrounded by fruit and vegetable venders hawking grapes, onions, coconut meat, peanuts, and anise seeds. Just inside the tenement is a small hallway, taken over by dogs, who seem to be either asleep or too weak to move. I stumble over their legs and heads, and go up a rickety staircase that smells of stale garlic. On the second floor, someone is furiously ringing a school bell; girls with thin little voices are milling about as if at a school; and someone is practicing scales on a saxophone. On the third floor, where Rajas lives in an end room, several men are lying or sitting on mats, and as I reach her door several chickens scatter.

Rajas's room seems small and suffocating, with hardly any space to move about. Some clothes hanging from a clothesline brush against my face. I duck, and get to the other side of the clothesline, only to come up against a crib hanging from the ceiling and some benches jammed against the bed. A woman is sitting on the bed. She is Rajas.

"Who is it?" she asks. "I have invited you in, but I can't tell who you are."

I introduce myself, but it takes her a long time to register who I am. She invites me to sit down on a bench. She is thrilled, but only momentarily, for she almost immediately begins complaining about hard times. "I have three children to support," she says. "Come here, child. Say hello to your uncle."

A girl of about seven, who has been clattering around in the far corner with some kitchen utensils, comes up to me and stiffly hugs my leg and says in a little voice, "Hello, Uncle." She goes back to the far corner.

I ask Rajas if she remembers anything about me at school.

"I remember that you were a very jolly child," she says.

I press her for details, but except for that phrase her memory yields nothing. But my memory yields even less, for I can't remember her at all.

When I try to get her to talk about our school days, she says she doesn't remember anything. I feel frustrated and angry, but then I remember my near-total loss of Marathi and feel sad for her—sad for both of us.

I get up to leave.

Suddenly, she starts whining like a street beggar. "Bountiful Sahib, a Braille watch. Something to tell the time with, for your poor Rajas. I've never had a watch. From you, as you can send. One Braille watch for your poor blind friend."

I stay long enough to assure her that I know her address, and then I practically run out of her room, and bolt down the stairs and out, almost falling over chickens, men, children, and dogs—her begging tone having stirred up a still earlier memory and an old fear.